Reclaiming the Church Family

Reclaiming the Church Family

A Solution to the Corporate-Church Crisis

MATTHEW T. KIMBROUGH

WIPF & STOCK · Eugene, Oregon

RECLAIMING THE CHURCH FAMILY
A Solution to the Corporate-Church Crisis

Wipf & Stock
An Imprint of Wipf and Stock Publishers
199 W. 8th Ave., Suite 3
Eugene, OR 97401

www.wipfandstock.com

PAPERBACK ISBN: 978-1-6667-3048-7
HARDCOVER ISBN: 978-1-6667-2208-6
EBOOK ISBN: 978-1-6667-2209-3

01/06/22

Contents

Preface

THE STORY OF THIS book begins near a dumpster in a hotel parking lot on the outskirts of Memphis. There, I traversed my own Damascus road (see Acts 9). Unlike the apostle Paul, I didn't travel to Memphis to attack Christians or destroy a church. I moved there to become a rock star.

My dad worked in vocational ministry as an associate pastor and, unfortunately, served under some poor examples of what a senior pastor should be. As a result of one of the bad times, my family left Southeast Missouri the summer before my seventh-grade year. After loading our boxes onto the rental truck, I lingered in the church parsonage we had called home, waiting until only I remained. The message I left on the bathroom mirror—unbeknownst to my parents until I finally admitted it in my late twenties—summed up my attitude toward pastoral ministry for years to come: "I hate you." (I've always wondered who found my postscript. Did they think it was the work of the devil trying to discourage them? Or worse, did they think my dad did it?)

We attended only two churches in our new town. The second, Springhill Baptist Church, became my family. Over twenty years later, I still worship every week with my Springhill family. I prize Springhill, and, if God allows, I will never leave. Through Springhill, God healed my brokenness and called me to a greater purpose—a lifetime of ministry. Unfortunately, rock music was playing too loudly in my ears to hear God at first, so I went to Memphis to pursue a career as a Christian musician. God responded by blessing me with misery. Misery came not from any failure on the part of the worship arts college or because of the rinky-dink hotel we called our dorm. I loved what I was learning but hated every minute I lived in Memphis.

Deep down, I think I knew I had chosen the wrong path. Like the prophet Jonah, God blessed me with misery to veer me back toward the road he had prepared.

God struck me one night while I took the trash out to the hotel-dorm dumpster. I heard no audible voice and felt no tangible pinch, but the message was clear. "I want you to give your life to the church," God said. I soon phoned my girlfriend (now my wife) to tell her that I thought God wanted me to become a pastor—the last thing I ever desired to be. But, I knew God had called me, and I had to follow.

A week later, my brother visited me in Memphis. I knew that if I didn't jump ship while he was there, I never would. So, I abruptly dropped out of college. We crammed my meager belongings into his car and drove the five hours back home. For years after, I refused to utter the name Memphis. To this day, my family refers to Memphis as "the city that shall not be named." Still, I wouldn't change those six weeks if I had a time machine. Through my misery, God gave me a purpose, and he continues to refine it to this day. God's patient guidance over the next decade of my life is a story worth telling, but it will have to wait. Suffice it to say, God allowed me to serve as one of the pastors of Springhill a few years later, and they haven't been able to get rid of me since.

After twenty years, my affection continues to grow for my brothers and sisters at Springhill. They are the laboratory where I have tested the thesis of this book—that the church is a family. Most recently, the small group Emily and I lead has allowed me to reshape what it looks like to live as a family under Christ. Because of them, I believe with utter conviction that churches today can become families and thrive as a result.

By God's grace, our parents are also family in Christ. My parents, Max and Andrea, and my mother-in-law, Missy, constantly demonstrate faithful servanthood in the family of God. Even the selfless servanthood of my late father-in-law continues to echo through the halls of Springhill every time deacons or Sunday School leaders gather. I strive to imitate them as they imitate Christ. And in a book about siblings, I have to admit that I have learned more from mine on both sides of our family than they have from me. Nathan, Jennie, Kali, and Kyle have shaped my idea of siblingship more than any book or article. Without them, this book would not exist.

I dedicate this book to those who day by day teach me the most: my wife and kids. My closest sister in Christ, my wife Emily, supports, encourages, challenges, and blesses me both with and without words. She is both the scalpel God continually uses to remove the cancer of sin in my life and the God-given morphine that allows me to bear the pain of sanctification. She is a kind, generous, and joyful woman who loves Christ deeply, and I'm glad to call her my partner. My children, Rylie and Koen, have contributed more to my pastoral theology than any textbook or seminary class ever did. They teach me about my relationship to the Father in ways that only a child could. I am truly blessed.

Finally, I'm thankful to the Father who has adopted me into his family by the death and resurrection of my brother, Jesus. Any growth you experience as you read comes from him. And any praise for the words that follow belongs to God alone.

Abreviations

BECNT Baker Exegetical Commentary on the New Testament
JSNTSS Journal for the Study of the New Testament Supplement Series
LCL Loeb Classical Library
LNTS Library of New Testament Studies
NIVAC NIV Application Commentary
TNTC Tyndale New Testament Commentary

1

Introduction

The Power of a Metaphor

THE CHURCH IS A family, not a business. Church leaders are pastors, not CEOs. Members are siblings, not colleagues. I intend to explore these claims in the pages that follow. But do such distinctions really matter? So what if our pastor sees himself as a corporate executive. As long as he accomplishes his weekly tasks—preaching, counseling, and organizing—and the church fulfills its obligations—evangelism and discipleship—should we split hairs over terminology? In other words, is this book worthy of my time?

Yes, it is! In case my answer doesn't satisfy you, let's look at the facts. The familial metaphor appears in twenty-five of the twenty-seven New Testament books. Every New Testament author except Jude calls followers of Jesus *siblings*.[1] And when the original New Testament audiences thought of a brother or sister, they didn't imagine someone they called once a week. They thought of siblings as deeply connected, loyal, and affectionate family members. Siblings protect one another. They encourage and correct. And they work hard to preserve their relationship. And the New Testament expects fellow believers to do the same. Not every author emphasizes the siblingship of believers to the same degree, but sibling language quickly

---

1. This statistic includes both singular and plural occurrences.

1

became the standard way to describe the church.[2] So, this book is worthy of your time if you desire your local church to conform to the image of church life we see in Scripture.[3]

Before we jump into Scripture, though, we need to understand the importance of metaphors. Why does it matter that the New Testament so frequently employs familial metaphors? If metaphors are mere analogies meant to entertain an audience, then the prominence of sibling language doesn't hold much weight for our churches today. They used some metaphors, and we use others. No harm, no foul. But if metaphors dramatically alter how we think and, as a result, determine how we act, then metaphors matter. So, hang with me as we briefly discuss the sneaky power of the metaphor.

FRIEND, TEACHER, WARDEN, OR COACH?

The Christian Scriptures lay down the law on marriage. Leave and cleave (Gen 2:24). Don't divorce (Matt 19:9). Husbands must love their wives as Christ loves the church, and wives should respect their husbands (Eph 5:28–33). Paul even prohibits married couples from pursuing holiness through celibacy (1 Cor 7:2–5). But when it comes to parenting, the waters become murky. Proverbs celebrates fatherly discipline as an act of love, and Paul warns fathers not to irritate their children needlessly (Col 3:21).[4] But where is the biblical book devoted to clear, direct parenting guidelines?

Today, parenting blogs fill the vacuum of Scripture's relative silence on the hows and whens of raising children. New mothers and fathers desperate to locate a rescue raft on the raging river of dirty diapers and all-night crying sessions (for the infant and parents) cling to parenting blogs. At least someone can give a solution at three in the morning when the real trouble begins. The problem, though, is that bloggers disagree—not just about specific strategies but about the foundation of parenting. At the heart of their disagreement is the *root metaphor* for parenting. In other words, what image should we use to describe the parent-child relationship? Is the parent a friend? A teacher? A prison warden? A life coach? What exactly *is* a parent?

---

2. See the bibliography for resources that note the importance of familial metaphors in Old and New Testament theology.

3. Most New Testament texts address a localized gathering of believers such as the church in Thessalonica. We cannot deny the overlap between the local, visible church and the universal, invisible church, but my emphasis throughout the book will be on the local church. I think of the universal church like those family members you see only at family reunions or on Facebook. They're still family, but not the kind you depend on every day.

4. See also Heb 12:9–10.

Such questions may sound philosophical and abstract, but the practical implications matter. Parents whose root metaphor is warden inevitably make their children into prisoners. The warden strives to produce children who obey the rules, and insubordination is the ultimate crime. Contrast the life coach root metaphor. Life coaches guide their children with words of encouragement, so little Jack and Jill can reach their personal goals. Life coaches don't set the agenda or demand obedience. They practice a soft touch, gently buffering their children along the path to success.

I doubt many parents consciously articulate their root metaphor. And most mix and match metaphors as needed, an essential practice for the challenging and endlessly fluctuating task of parenting. Good parents seamlessly shift from coach to teacher to drill sergeant without grinding their gears. The problem comes when parents latch onto a single root metaphor and don't let go—especially when they don't realize it. Wardens mindlessly scream at their children without remorse and demand compliance without grace because their primary image of what a parent *is* does not allow mercy. Children can't step outside the house—the penitentiary—because the warden can't trust them. The subconscious root metaphor becomes a filter for all parenting decisions and attitudes because how parents think about their role determines everything they do.

THINKING BEGETS DOING

The apostle Paul also believed that the way people think determines what they do. Paul frames the theologically rich epistle to the Romans around the issue of *thinking*. Paul begins the letter in 1:18–32 with idolatry—the creature worshiping fellow creatures rather than the Creator. God's response is judgment, though not the kind often depicted in popular culture. God doesn't threaten to strike down profane sinners with a lightning bolt. No, God offers an even more alarming response, essentially telling the sinner, "Thy will be done."

Specifically, Paul describes three ways God hands over sinners to their sin, enacting what we might call passive judgment. Parents practice passive judgment by permitting their daughter to wear those sparkly but uncomfortable shoes on a hike, allowing natural consequences to teach the lesson. Active judgment, on the other hand, looks like grounding the teen who misses curfew.

Paul begins his discussion of sin and judgment in Romans with a sequence of passive judgments against those who idolize fellow creatures. God hands idolaters over to their impurity (v. 24) and then to degrading passions (v. 26). But God reserves the third act of passive punishment for those who refuse even to acknowledge God's existence: God gives them over to a depraved mind (v. 28). Depraved thinking produces a litany of sinful behaviors (vv. 29–31) and causes sinners to celebrate the sinfulness of others (v. 32). The depraved mind sets no boundaries on depraved actions, and utter sinfulness inevitably follows.

Thankfully, Paul doesn't end his epistle after chapter 1. We can't discuss the entire epistle, but two other pit stops will illustrate the value the apostle places on thinking. First, let's jump to Romans 6:11, the middle of the primarily theological portion of the letter. Before chapter 6, Paul explains that the only hope for both Jews and Gentiles is to have faith in the atoning work of Christ (Romans 1–4), who has righted the wrongs of Adam and overcome sin with grace (chapter 5). Now, believers fully unite with Christ in his death and resurrection, so they may honestly claim, "The old me is dead."

In light of the believer's union with Christ, Paul issues a command in Romans 6:11 (NASB), "Even so consider yourselves to be dead to sin, but alive to God in Christ Jesus." The verb *consider* (*logizesthe*) is the first imperative verb in the entire book of Romans addressed to the audience. In all of Paul's discussions about homosexuality, pride, faith, division, righteousness, and more, he never uses an imperative verb to call his audience to action, not until now.[5] And what is the command he saves until halfway through the letter? "Think this way!" The verb comes from the world of math: sit and calculate this reality.[6] No longer may the Roman church exemplify depraved thinking that produces depraved living. They must think of themselves as dead to sin (by joining Jesus in his death) and then live like it (see Rom 6:12–23).

One more stop in Romans will complete our brief journey. We saw depraved thinking as a passive punishment in Rom 1. In chapter 6, Paul claimed that thinking about the believer's union with Christ overcomes the power of sin. Now, let's jump to the point of transition between the theologically heavy portion of the letter (chs. 1–11) and a practical section that applies the truth of the gospel (chs. 12–16). The famous transition appears in Romans 12:1–2. Paul writes, "Therefore I urge you, brethren, by the mercies of God, to present your bodies a living and holy sacrifice, acceptable to God, which is your spiritual service of worship. And do not be conformed to this world, but *be transformed by the renewing of your mind, so that you may prove what the will of God is, that which is good and acceptable and perfect*"

---

5. Admittedly, he does use other grammatical structures with a similar effect.

6. The verb is often translated "reckon" in Rom 4, where it plays a key role in Paul's argument.

(NASB, emphasis added). Paul's instructions are pregnant with meaning, but let's focus on verse 2. Believers don't avoid conformity to the world by meeting regularly with an accountability partner or practicing the spiritual disciplines with rigidity, at least not according to Paul. Worldly thinking is the problem, so a renewed mind is the only solution. Only transformed thinking prepares believers to live in a way that is good, acceptable, and perfect.

In all, Romans demonstrates the consequence of human thought patterns. God allows those who deny him to wallow in depraved thinking, leading to all sorts of sins. But the remedy to living as slaves to sin begins with mental redirection: think of yourselves (as you really are!) as dead to sin but alive to God in Christ Jesus. The underlying problem of ethnic division in the church is also foremost cognitive. The Christian community must renew its collective mind by recognizing the essential unity of the body of Christ. Paul's underlying assumption is that thinking begets doing.

THE POWER OF A ROOT

"Fine," you may be saying aloud to this book, "you provided anecdotal evidence (parenting blogs) and biblical evidence (Romans), but do modern social scientists agree? Can they corroborate that the way churches think of themselves will affect everything they do?" Thank you for asking. Cognitive linguists explain that metaphors allow people to conceptualize abstract ideas and make sense of their lives. In their famous work on cognitive linguistics, *Metaphors We Live By*, Lakoff and Johnson contend, "Metaphor is pervasive in everyday life, not just in language but in thought and action. Our ordinary conceptual system, in terms of which we both think and act, is fundamentally metaphorical in nature."[7] Metaphors connect the mental dots in life to draw coherent images of the world around us.

Using Root Metaphors

Take the abstract concept of *love*. How can we explain something as mysterious as love? Popular lyricists use metaphors. Dolly Parton's 1974 album titled *Love Is Like a Butterfly* compared romance to the gentlest of creatures. Somewhat less appealing is Duke Ellington's song titled "Love Is Like a Cigarette." And we haven't even touched on modern country music yet. My point

---

7. Lakoff and Johnson, *Metaphors We Live By*, 1.

is that metaphors allow us to use familiar, concrete images—butterflies and cigarettes—to understand abstract concepts such as love.

Bible scholars also recognize the importance of foundational root metaphors. We find root metaphors buried deep in our mental soil, nourishing metaphorical branches that shoot off in many directions. In her article on the ethical implications of metaphors in the Revelation, Susan Hylen describes the power of root metaphors, writing, "Metaphors invite the reader into a way of seeing the world. Even a common, conventional metaphor asks the reader or hearer to take an imaginative leap, to envision the world in a particular way."[8] Because root metaphors influence how we think about the important things in life, flawed or strained metaphors are all the more dangerous.

Abusing Root Metaphors

Let's zoom in a bit further before we return to the topic at hand. Lakoff and Johnson pioneered the idea that metaphors link a concept such as *time* with a concrete image like *money*. The way metaphors work is that the idea and concrete image have specific, limited points of correspondence.

Aspects of the Concrete Image: Money	Correspondence with Concept: Time	Phrase Expressing a Conceptual Link between Time and Money
Valuable	Yes	"Time with my kids is precious."
Saving so that more is available later	Yes	"I saved time by working through lunch so I could have more time to relax."
Borrowing from others	Yes	"Can I borrow a minute of your time to tell you about a product?"
Getting a refund	No	
Purchasing using credit	No	

As you see in the table, several correspondence points between time and the root metaphor of money make the comparison helpful. Time, like money, is valuable. People save time to spend it elsewhere. Despite points of correspondence, though, the concept and the metaphor are by no means equivalent. The idea of a time credit card is preposterous. What would time

---

8. Hylen, "Metaphor Matters," 783. Hylen laments that violent metaphors became embedded in the Christian imagination, reaping a path of aggression throughout church history.

interest rates even mean? Do we have a time collections agency? Can we declare time bankruptcy and reset the clock somehow? The absurdity created by a false point of correspondence proves that we shouldn't overextend the root metaphor.

Metaphors operate like powerful mental software that processes the abstract ones and zeros that make up our lives. Unfortunately, software can become corrupt, and a corrupt metaphor can be harmful. The real damage comes when we think wrongly about a concept by expanding the metaphor beyond its boundaries. Back to Hylen's argument, the letters to the seven churches in Revelation 2–3 call believers to overcome, a battle image derived from the root metaphor that depicts faith as a war. The image suggests that believers face spiritual warfare and must fight tooth and nail to persevere. Yet, in the Middle Ages, Christian crusaders overextended the root metaphor beyond the realm of spiritual battles to include physical combat against unconverted peoples, and the results were disastrous.[9] Metaphor abuse can become a serious crime.

I contend that metaphor abuse is harming our churches. We have overplayed the points of correspondence between *church* and *business*. Now, the corporate-church model has distorted the rich colors of biblical ecclesiology (the doctrine of the church), leaving behind a colorless, unappealing organization instead of a vibrant, indispensable family. Therefore, the goal of this book is to rescue the better root metaphor from the trash heap, reclaiming the church as a family. Like the talented restoration artists who worked diligently to remove soot and candle wax from Michelangelo's Sistine Chapel frescoes, I hope to scrape away the grime obscuring the beauty of Christ's bride. And with a Scripture-shaped paintbrush, we will retouch the portrait of our congregations to display our Father proudly.

JESUS, THE FAMILY MAN

In the pages that follow, we will uncover family language hiding in plain sight throughout the New Testament epistles. Yet, sibling language begins with Jesus. So as an appetizer, let's consider a few key passages in Matthew's Gospel that introduce Christ-followers as the family of God. In these passages, we will set the stage for our later chapters with four foundational commands:

- Don't attack siblings.
- Resolve conflict humbly.

9. Hylen, "Metaphor Matters."

- Make the church family a priority.
- Don't imitate the world's version of leadership.

Don't Attack Siblings

When Jesus taught his followers about conflict, he sprinkled in sibling language. The Sermon on the Mount provides valuable examples. Early in the sermon, Jesus redefines several of the Ten Commandments to get at the heart of God's ancient instructions. Jesus says that when God prohibited murder, he also included anger, especially toward a brother. I don't advocate acting in anger toward anyone, but I also want to spotlight the word we gloss over in the following passage: *brother*. Matthew 5:22 (NASB) says, "But I say to you that everyone who is angry with his brother shall be guilty before the court; and whoever says to his brother, 'You good-for-nothing,' shall be guilty before the supreme court; and whoever says, 'You fool,' shall be guilty enough to go into the fiery hell." According to Jesus, even the simplest attack against a sibling ("You fool!") is as intolerable as murder. Relationships in the family of God require high standards of personal conduct.

To illustrate, Jesus teaches that a worshipper who remembers a conflict with his brother while presenting an offering to God should leave, seeking to restore the relationship immediately. Jesus concludes in Matt 5:34b (NASB), "First be reconciled to your brother, and then come and present your offering." While I have instigated conflicts with many siblings, I am ashamed to admit that I have never fled a worship service to seek reconciliation. I imagine I am not the only one who has quietly neglected Jesus's explicit instruction while claiming to worship God faithfully. But we cannot separate our worship from our relationships with fellow believers, any more than the naked eye can distinguish between the hydrogen and oxygen molecules in water. God demands worship that is vertical and horizontal.

Resolve Conflict Humbly

Later in the Sermon on the Mount, Jesus prohibits prideful believers from critiquing the problems of their spiritual siblings. Matthew 7:3–5 records the ironic analogy of a brother with a wooden post protruding from his eye who focuses not on his own traumatic injury but on his sibling's minor eye irritation. The brother blinded by his own sin—the one wearing the fence post—can't see clearly enough to condemn others, but that doesn't stop him.

Jesus's story reminds me of an adventure race show I watched recently. One team leader screamed instructions from the foot of a sheer mountain face, telling a tired teammate to climb more efficiently. When his turn arrived, he exhausted his muscles immediately because, after all the time he spent giving advice, he didn't know how to use the equipment (much to my amusement). I'm amazed by our inability as humans to judge ourselves properly. We base our self-confidence and right to critique on absolutely nothing. But this silly human tendency didn't surprise Jesus. And while he might have applied his critique to any relationship, he chose siblings.

Society applies this passage to support the "don't judge me" mantra so popular today. But believers recognize our obligation to confront sin and false teaching among our spiritual family (compare Matt 7:15–20; 1 Cor 5). How do we judge, then, without judging? Better yet, how do we protect one another from sin without becoming judgmental? We acknowledge that God has not given us the ministry of condemnation (Rom 12:19) but of reconciliation (2 Cor 5:18). We critique out of love, desiring the best for our family (Gal 6:1). And we freely admit our faults to one another (Jas 5:16).[10] The messiness of our relationships with fellow Christians demands that we begin this book with a healthy dose of reality. Reclaiming the family of God won't happen overnight but will require hours of heartache and hard work. Because of sin, conflict is, was, and will always be part of the normal human experience, even in the family of God.

One of the most well-known passages on Christian conflict is Matthew 18:15–35. The two subsections both begin by referring to brothers, and Jesus concludes with a warning of judgment (v. 35 NASB): "My heavenly Father will also do the same to you, if each of you does not forgive his brother from your heart." Jesus teaches his followers to act humbly, seeking a conversation with an offending brother in a way that protects him from unnecessary embarrassment. It begins with a one-on-one conversation and adds other voices only if necessary. If the brother responds, you must forgive him and keep forgiving as a living parable of the gospel. Forgiven people forgive others.

In all, then, the root metaphor of Christian siblingship provides an essential foundation for Christian reconciliation. Co-workers aren't bound to forgive one another endlessly. Acquaintances won't look in the mirror before condemning one another. Even close friends fall prey to name-calling

---

10. Tverberg, *Walking in the Dust*, 114, sums it up well: "While you can discern sin in practice, only God knows the whole motive of the heart. We can (and should) discern outward wrongdoing, but we aren't qualified to slam down the gavel and declare God's condemnation on the person as a whole."

(although "You fool!" isn't our go-to anymore). But the family of God should be different.

Make the Church Family a Priority

In addition to discussion about conflict, Jesus shockingly treats his spiritual family as his primary kin. We will discuss the priority of the ancient family in a later chapter. Still, even the most cursory reading reveals how offended Jesus's blood relatives would have felt during conversations like the one recorded in Matthew 12:46–50. In a seemingly mundane moment, Jesus's mother and earthly siblings seek him out. But rather than acknowledge them, he uses the moment to teach his followers about their kinship with one another. The passage concludes in v. 50 (NASB) when Jesus says, "For whoever does the will of My Father who is in heaven, he is My brother and sister and mother." What a slap in the face! I would never tell my son and daughter that the college students I teach are my true children. But Jesus doesn't hold back. Keep in mind that Joseph had likely died, leaving Jesus, the oldest son, as the head of the family. Mary, James, and Jesus's other blood relatives must have felt orphaned by his single-minded commitment to the family of God—his followers. Still, Jesus thought it was worth the pain his lesson would inflict to teach the disciples that they were family.

Jesus also anticipated that his disciples would sacrifice relationships to follow him. In parts of the world today, we still see new converts disowned by their relatives for following Christ. But Jesus promises believers will regain all they have lost, including family. Matthew 19:29 (NASB) says, "And everyone who has left houses or brothers or sisters or father or mother or children or farms for My name's sake, will receive many times as much, and will inherit eternal life." I cannot imagine the loss a disowned new believer must feel, but the family he gains is much greater. In some ways, our Christian siblings are a sort of consolation for the sacrifices required for Christ-followers. The family of God, then, isn't a mere illustration. It is a concrete new reality for those who profess faith in Jesus. We are a family.

Don't Imitate the World's Version of Leadership

Another passage in Matthew anticipates how the early church will organize itself. Jesus critiques certain Pharisees for the self-centered ways they lead their followers. They pursue their own renown and refuse to help people struggling to live up to their standards. They also imitate the rest of the world in their vain pursuit of personal honor, so Jesus strongly warns his disciples not to imitate them. In Matthew 23:8–10 (NASB), Jesus cautions, "But do not be called Rabbi; for One is your Teacher, and you are all brothers. Do not call anyone on earth your father; for One is your Father, He who is in heaven. Do not be called leaders; for One is your Leader, that is, Christ." These commands will prevent the disciples from imitating systems where hierarchies devalue those on the lower rungs of the ladder. Jesus rejects the exalted leader, even the celebrity teacher. Leadership in the family of God belongs first, foremost, and almost entirely to the triune God. Those who serve as pastors and ministers are instruments in God's hand, not rulers of our own kingdoms.

Given Jesus's emphasis on the spiritual family, which would become the church, we should not be surprised that the remainder of the New Testament follows suit. The book of Acts includes dozens of references to Christian siblings. Paul uses familial language in key theological and practical passages. Hebrews 2 even builds a doctrine of Christ on a familial foundation. From the beginning of Matthew to Rev 19:10, sibling language permeates the New Testament, planting a root metaphor that blossomed in the early church. In this book, I hope that a rainstorm of honest critique and bright rays of biblical hope will awaken a dormant seed that can bear great fruit in our churches. How's that for a metaphor?

WHAT TO EXPECT MOVING FORWARD

If you're in the market for another church-bashing tirade, you've picked up the wrong book. I write out of love and longing for what the church can become after a potentially painful pruning process. This book is not 99 percent critique and 1 percent solution. In fact, we divide each chapter into three sections. First, we will examine what happens "If the Church Is a Business." The first step in each chapter will be to consider evidence of the corporate-church model and its negative implications. The first section will be heavy on critique. Second, we'll look to Scripture to see what happens "If the Church Is a Family." The goal of section 2 is to dig deeply into the biblical text, where we'll notice a consistent metaphorical thread depicting believers as siblings in the family of God. We'll also consider the benefits of living as a Christian family. The third section, "Swapping Metaphors," will suggest how to return to the biblical image. How can our churches slowly and realistically change? What are potential hindrances? And how will a commitment to the family model impact church life?

Along the way, four ideas will guide our journey:

- At least one correspondence between the business and church worlds produced a root metaphor that pictures the church as a business. For example, most churches hire and fire employees the same as any company must.

- Church members and leaders often draw additional points of correspondence between church and business that are harmful, like the tendency of church members to act like consumers.

- A more biblical and less perilous root metaphor depicts the church as a family.

- By consciously examining these root metaphors and exalting the better one, we can diagnose and treat some of the ills that plague modern church life.

On this journey, I encourage you to read prayerfully and with your Bible in hand. My intent is not to offer practical advice drawn from my successful gambit as a ministry leader. Instead, I want to draw us back to Scripture as the foundation for all we do—including church life. Let's allow God's word to reshape our thinking and, as a result, inspire us to reconnect as brothers and sisters in Christ.

2

Insights, Not a Paradigm

The Role of Business Practices in Church Life

We are unapologetically attractional. In our search for common ground with unchurched people, we've discovered that, like us, they are consumers. So we leverage their consumer instincts. By the way, if your church has heating and air conditioning, you do too. When you read the Gospels, it's hard to overlook the fact that Jesus attracted large crowds everywhere he went. He was constantly playing to the consumer instincts of his crowds. Let's face it: It wasn't the content of his messages that appealed to the masses.

—ANDY STANLEY

WHEN WE ARRIVED IN Springfield, Missouri, late in the summer of 1998, the search for a church was on. We knew a revival preacher who attended Springhill Baptist Church, so we visited on our second Sunday in town. I can't speak for my parents, but I'm confident I was their focus when choosing a church. My brother was entering his senior year of high school, so he wouldn't be part of the youth ministry for long. I, on the other hand, would soon start seventh grade. The church we joined would play a formative role in my Christian life—a reality I'm sure my parents recognized.

My parents considered Springhill's theology, preaching ministry, and leadership structure. The church's numerical growth certainly didn't escape them, nor did the senior pastor's popularity. But I'm pretty sure the reason we stayed was because of Andy, Emma, and Jana. These three Springhill members weren't deacons, pastors, or staff members. They were three seventh graders who, Sunday after Sunday, kept inviting me to sit with them during the worship service. I can't recall how many times I said no before Andy, Emma, and Jana wore me down. But once I gave in, the Kimbroughs were hooked. Truthfully, I needed more than a well-structured organization with good teaching and engaging music. I needed a family. Three fellow seventh graders gave me a glimpse of what Springhill could be. Everything I have done in ministry and any spiritual growth I have experienced since the summer of 1998 traces back to them.

In this first chapter, I want to set the stage for the book with a positive note. The business world is not irrelevant to church life. We can learn something from watching good business leaders, just as we can learn from watching children play hide and seek. So, I want to prevent the pendulum I'm pushing from flying off its hinges. Yet, the New Testament authors can't help but use family language—not business terminology—when writing about the church. And if the root metaphor "the church is a family" is so engrained in their thinking, it must have been the underlying paradigm for understanding the purpose and function of the church.

IF THE CHURCH IS A BUSINESS: CONSUMERS, COMPETITION, AND COMMUNICATORS

I am tempted to save this chapter for the end of the book. Launch an all-out blitzkrieg against the corporate-church model, and then wave the flag of peace at the end. The strategy is a sensible one, but I must take a different tactic.

Wisdom from the Business World

Insights from the business world can benefit the church. I am not naïve or idealistic enough to ignore this truth. God has graciously provided an orderly world that we can observe for the sake of gaining wisdom. The book of Proverbs proves the point. In essence, Proverbs records observations from everyday life that teach those who fear the Lord how to live (or how not to live). One of my favorite proverbs records a repulsive habit in nature that remains common nearly three millennia later. "Like a dog that returns to its vomit / Is a fool who repeats his folly" (Proverbs 26:11 NASB).

Of the three spoiled canines my wife and I have had, Willy illustrated the proverb regularly. Willy squeezed into my parents' garage as a starving puppy three weeks before my wife and I got married. We fed him, and he refused to leave. Willy was always the kind of dog who couldn't be trusted around food. If I dumped a fifty-pound bag of dog food on the ground, Willy would eat until he burst. So, I saw Willy fulfill the proverb on more than one occasion.

By observing the world around us, we can notice repetitive or unusual behaviors and draw implications from them.[1] Observation is the work of the sage. Solomon and the other authors of Proverbs were sages who mined the world around them for whatever precious jewels of wisdom they could find. One diamond in the rough was the ferociously hungry dog that wasn't sensible enough to forsake the food his body once rejected and, instead, chose to ingest it again—likely producing the same outcome. The sage, noticing this unfortunate tendency, ponders that few humans would willingly eat what their bodies had violently discharged. But a fool is just as contradictory when he makes the same mistake twice. And so the proverb was born.

Let me, then, restate this truth: God has graciously provided an orderly world that we can observe for the sake of gaining wisdom. And if a disgusting canine habit can impart wisdom, surely an observant Christian can gain insight from successful businesses. Therefore, we cannot claim that looking to the business world for wisdom is unbiblical. I truly believe this was the initial desire of the pastoral leadership movement. "If we can utilize successful business models," they thought, "to build large, wealthy, organized churches, we can reach more people with the good news of Jesus Christ." Returning to the quote at the beginning of this chapter, we see a tenderhearted goal. Andy Stanley recalls, "In our search for common ground with unchurched people, we've discovered that, like us, they are consumers. So we leverage their consumer instincts."[2] Andy's noble purpose is to reach unbelievers—a mission we should all applaud.

The Paradigm Problem

A problem arises, though, when a source of wisdom becomes a paradigm—a root metaphor. Let's return to the vomit-eating dog. The sage may learn a valuable lesson from such a creature. Only one correspondence point relates

1. In fact, scholars discovered the idea of a root metaphor by such a process.
2. Stanley, *Deep and Wide*, 16.

to the proverb: making the same mistake twice is like returning to consume your vomit. Beyond the proverb, a creative thinker could add other correspondences between a dog and humans. People benefit from regular exercise (daily walks). It's foolish to run away from a good home. And so on. But if I begin to see myself entirely through the *dog* lens, life will get weird. Should I sleep most of the day? Is it the responsibility of others to feed and bathe me? Must I yell at people who walk near my house? What is the correspondence between me and a dog that digs holes in the ground, drinks from the toilet, or constantly drools? What about chasing cats or despising postal workers?

My point is that while God may impart wisdom through a variety of means, we must be careful to protect the root metaphors that shape how we think and, as a result, determine how we live. True wisdom demands that we exalt only the root metaphors explicitly established in Scripture. Individually, we must confront our root metaphors—whether conscious or, more likely, subconscious—and convert them to biblical root metaphors. Otherwise, we will live foolishly because our thought patterns are inadequate.

If, at the individual level, a biblical root metaphor is essential, how much more critical is the lens through which we view the church. Our local churches represent millions of lives that desperately need a proper understanding of the church. Poor, unfounded, incomplete root metaphors for church life can harm generations of believers and prevent us from embodying the fullness of the church's mission. Therefore, my reason for standing against the overuse of business concepts in church life is because I believe the corporate-church root metaphor has unintentionally become the conceptual foundation for many American evangelical churches today. And this modern metaphor has the potential to cause more damage than good.

Before continuing, we must admit that few, if any, pastors or church members would ever say the phrase, "The church is a business, not a family." More to the point, I doubt any would deny that the church is a family to some extent. But, what are our underlying beliefs about church, the branches that extend from our root metaphor? What is the lens through which we view all facets of church life? What is our conceptual foundation, the thought pattern that determines how we view the purpose and structure of the church, the roles of church members and staff, even the reasons we gather? How do we define success and failure? Why should someone become involved in a church? I argue that our root metaphor will determine the answer to all of these questions and more. And from what I see, hear, and read, the primary root metaphor has become, "The church is a business."

A Deeply and Widely Held Metaphor

Since Andy Stanley's *Deep and Wide* is a highly influential book about the purpose of church, let's consider the implicit root metaphor undergirding the book. For clarity, I will italicize ideas that reveal the metaphor. First, we will return to the quote at the beginning of this chapter, where Stanley writes, "We are unapologetically *attractional*. In our search for common ground with unchurched people, we've discovered that, like us, they are *consumers*. So we leverage their *consumer instincts*. By the way, if your church has heating and air conditioning, you do too. When you read the Gospels, it's hard to overlook the fact that Jesus *attracted* large crowds everywhere he went. He was constantly playing to the *consumer instincts* of his crowds. Let's face it: It wasn't the content of his messages that appealed to the masses."[3] And again, "When we *launched* North Point, every other church in Atlanta was *competing* for the churched people *market*. We decided to get into the unchurched people *market*. That's a much larger *market* and we didn't have any *competition* at the time. If somebody liked our *brand*, we were the only *option*."[4]

The quotes above reveal two dangerous points of correspondence between the church and a business. First, those who come to our churches are consumers. As a consumer at Walmart, I don't enter the store to connect with other shoppers, encourage the employees, or better the organization. I come to get my paper towels at the lowest price possible, and then I hastily exit the store. I don't care whether the store succeeds or fails. If they close down, I'll just shop somewhere else. Do we want church members to think the same way?

Second, Andy Stanley implies that churches compete. How do I grow my church? I must find a market I can tap into because all churches compete for people and money. I fear the unbelieving world sees the unhealthy competitive streak between churches, and then they question the goodness of the gospel we preach. Nowhere in the New Testament do we see the idea that churches compete. But, this is a natural implication of the corporate-church model.

In case you still doubt whether this root metaphor holds sway, consider North Point's personnel decisions and how they reveal their root metaphor. Stanley writes, "Fortunately for us, there is a gentleman in our church, Brian Kaznova, who has helped us tremendously in this area. For the past several years, Brian has invested in our *organization* by designing *surveys* and then

---

3. Stanley, *Deep and Wide*, 16.
4. Stanley, *Deep and Wide*, 13.

providing *objective analysis* and recommendations based on the findings. Brian has extensive experience with *private corporations* consulting on *performance* and *organizational excellence*."[5]

Or take the following quotation. We could easily assume it came from an advertising agency rather than a church. Nothing in the following quote is distinctly Christian. "We've gone to great lengths to create a *system* that frees *communicators* and *content developers* to do what they do best. The corollary is we've gone to great lengths to protect our *audiences* from *presenters* who aren't *engaging*. We choose our most *engaging presenters*, give them great *content*, and then turn them loose. And we use those *presenters* in different *departments* throughout the *organization*."[6]

You may have missed that the quote you just read was about preaching! The *presenters* or *communicators* are preachers; the *audience* is a congregation; *content* is a sermon; and the *organization* is the church. More importantly, the assumption rooted in the business world is that success comes only through the most talented people. In the church context, the success of a sermon depends upon the presenters' skills. Yet, Paul declares that a rhetorically impressive presentation of the gospel risks invalidating its power. The apostle rejects rhetorical gymnastics, preferring to preach the simple message of Christ crucified (1 Cor 2:1–5). Paul was not nearly as pragmatic as modern ministry practitioners. But more on this later.

The final quote relates to North Point's church building: "If you standardize and quantify *great* for your ministry environments, evaluation becomes a way of life. It won't be limited to a meeting. Your entire organization will operate at higher standards with a lower threshold of tolerance for average."[7] The church leadership movement demands quantification. There is no success if it isn't numerically quantifiable. And yet, how do we quantify relational and spiritual growth? What numbers can reveal that God has defeated sin in a teenager's life or that a single mom loves Jesus more than she did this time last year? What data could show conclusively that church members care for the needs of the desperate among them? We must begin to ask these questions and consider what the answers reveal about the corporate-church model.

To be clear, I intend neither to criticize nor to demean Andy Stanley. I have no reason to believe he is anything short of a sincere pastor with an earnest concern for unbelievers. I will argue, though, that his root metaphor,

---

5. Stanley, *Deep and Wide*, 14.

6. Stanley, *Deep and Wide*, 178.

7. Stanley, *Deep and Wide*, 163 (emphasis in original).

"The church is a business," generates more problems than it solves. Even bananas, if they make up your entire diet, will eventually poison you.

Readers of *Deep and Wide* may not notice that the corporate-church paradigm permeates each page. Andy can't help but picture his church (or *organization*) in business terms. Since Andy holds incredible sway in the evangelical world, I'm not surprised to hear students, church members, and pastors from various churches around the nation speaking in Stanleyisms. I can't go to a conference without hearing about environments and markets. The church consulting industry continues to grow. And it seems that few are asking whether this is what church is supposed to be.

Potential Objections

Before turning to Scripture, I want to answer two retorts I often hear when broaching the subject of our root metaphor and its impact on church life. First, someone who doesn't want his view of the church critiqued may respond, "It's better to be a student than a critic. Don't attack. Just take what is helpful and leave the rest. Chew the meat and spit out the bones." Now, if ministry were simply a buffet of random skills and practices, this proverb would ring true. I like his speaking cadence, their youth ministry logo, that fun women's ministry event, and the way they structure support staff. So, I'll take those ideas and leave behind their service length and music volume because they don't appeal to me. I can be a student of the good without critiquing the bad. But since my concern is that pastors have built their houses on sand rather than rock, it isn't enough to be a student. It doesn't matter if the house has decorative windows and exquisite woodwork. I can't stop and admire the luxurious, ornate rugs because I urgently need to call a foundation repair specialist.

Since I am using Andy Stanley as a conversation partner, let me share my personal experience. During my time on staff at Springhill, I read several of Andy's pastoral leadership books. Our staff worked through *Deep and Wide* chapter by chapter during staff meetings. We even went to a ministry leaders conference at North Point Church in Atlanta. I listened to Andy defend his philosophy of ministry and heard his staff teach us how to do what they do. So, I have been a student. But as a Bible reader and as a pastor in a much smaller church, I found little I could hold on to. No, I don't have the funds to pay all of my nursery workers. More importantly, I can't swallow the picture of church life you're selling me. I just can't see it in Scripture. I walked away empty handed, jealous, frustrated, and searching.

This brings us to a second critique: you're just jealous. Fair enough. If we're honest, every staff member at smaller churches struggles with jealousy sometimes, and it is sinful. Like the husband who can't keep his eyes off other women, we watch booming ministries and assume the grass must be greener—that we could be happier elsewhere. We long for the respect and wealth that building a certain kind of church can give us. We think we have something to teach others, too, and we wish we had a platform to share our insights. In our worst moments, we deeply envy their "success." But, it is foolish to assume that every critique lodged against a megachurch is rooted in jealousy. More importantly, we shouldn't presume that only large churches suffer from the corporate-church crisis. The pastors of large churches write the books that influence the rest of us, so they're easy to critique. But the root metaphor is not determined by church size. A church of fifty members could have a distorted root metaphor just as a church of five thousand might. So, jealousy is not the driving force behind my critique. The biblical image of the church is.

IF THE CHURCH IS A FAMILY: WORDS MATTER

In their excellent book, *Misreading Scripture with Western Eyes*, E. Randolph Richards and Brandon J. O'Brien draw on their intercultural experiences to reveal how Western our reading of Scripture often is. One insight they offer relates to languages. They point out that while we have one word for rice in English, Indonesians have several. "In Indonesia there are fields of *padi*, bags of *beras* and plates of *nasi*."[8] On the other hand, we have multiple terms for the parts of a pig that we eat—bacon, ribs, chops, and roast—while those who don't eat pigs have only one word. Our words reveal what we value.

Church Words

When it comes to the "local collection of believers" or "all believers in all times and places," our favorite English word is *church* (*ekklesia* in Greek). If you use a concordance to look up the Greek word *ekklesia*, you'll find quite a few passages where the term refers to a local congregation.[9] Still, several

8. Richards and O'Brien, *Misreading Scripture with Western Eyes*, 73.

9. Matt 18:17; Acts 8:1; 11:22; 13:1; 14:23; 15:22, 41; 16:5; Rom 16:1, 4, 5, 16, 23; 1 Cor 1:2; 4:17; 7:17; 11:18; 14:4, 12, 19, 28, 33, 35; 16:1, 19; 2 Cor 1:1; 8:1, 18, 23; 11:8, 28; 12:13; Gal 1:2, 22; Phil 4:17; Col 4:15, 16; 1 Thess 1:1; 2:14; 2 Thess 1:1; 1 Tim 3:5, 15; 5:16; Phlm 2; Jas 5:14; 3 John 6, 9; Rev 1:4, 11, 20; 2:1, 7, 8, 11, 12, 17, 18, 23, 29; 3:1, 6, 7, 13, 14, 22; 22:16. We might also add a few passages in Ephesians to the list. But in

New Testament books are missing. Well over one-third of the New Testament books do not call a local collection of believers a *church*.[10] We could forgive Mark, Luke, and John, since the full vision of the church doesn't appear until the book of Acts. But what about 2 Timothy and Titus? These books are two-thirds of the collection we usually call the Pastoral Epistles, and the word *church* is conspicuously absent. You may have also noticed that once we step outside of Paul's epistles, we don't see much reference to the church at all—at least not using that term.

Before we draw the wrong conclusion, let's be clear. Every New Testament book is concerned with the church. In the Gospels, Jesus anticipates church life when he teaches the disciples how to become servants, using his sacrificial ministry as a prime example. In Acts and the epistles, we see the church taking shape and plodding forward through victories and failures. Revelation depicts the triumph of the church over the enemy and his forces. But church is not the primary word, especially for a local gathering of believers. Instead, the king of all terms for the local church is *brothers*.

All but two of the New Testament books use the plural *brothers* for a group of believers in Jesus. No other church word or phrase is so pervasive. Every inspired New Testament author, except Jude in his twenty-five-verse-long epistle,[11] pictures gatherings of believers as a family. Not friends, colleagues, co-workers, partners, customers, or even members. Believers in Jesus are brothers.

In case the ladies are wondering about their role in the Christian fraternity, humor me for a moment as we discuss Greek. The Greek word for brother is *adelphos* (think Phil*adelphia*, the city of brotherly love). In the plural, *adelphos* can refer to a group of men only or a mixed group of men and women. This is normal in languages where all nouns have a gender. For example, Acts 1:15 uses *the brothers* to describe the first church gathering of about 120 people in Jerusalem. In the prior two verses, Luke depicts the mixed composition of this group, writing, "When they had entered the city, they went up to the upper room where they were staying; that is, Peter and John and James and Andrew, Philip and Thomas, Bartholomew and Matthew, James the son of Alphaeus, and Simon the Zealot, and Judas the son of James. These all with one mind were continually devoting themselves to prayer, *along with the women*, and *Mary the mother of Jesus*, and with His

---

Ephesians, Paul seems to be talking universally, especially in ch. 5, where he dubs the church the bride of Christ.

10. Twelve out of twenty-seven do not use *ekklesia* in a local sense: Mark, Luke, John, Ephesians, 2 Timothy, Titus, Hebrews, 1 Peter, 2 Peter, 1 John, 2 John, and Jude.

11. The books of Titus and Jude do not use the term *brothers*, preferring terms like believers, the elect ones, and the beloved ones.

brothers. At this time Peter stood up in the midst of *the brethren* (a gathering of about one hundred and twenty persons was there together)" (Acts 1:13–15 NASB, emphasis added).

Luke uses *brothers* (or, for the stodgier among us, *brethren*) for a mixed group of believers—men and women. So the Christian Standard Bible rightly translates, "In those days Peter stood up among the *brothers and sisters*."[12] Native Greek speakers would happily endorse this translation without a second thought. So, throughout this book, I will use the more neutral *sibling(s)*, *brothers and sisters*, or the generic *brothers* for *adelphos* when appropriate in the biblical context.

What Kind of Siblings?

Maybe you think that while sibling language sounds nice, you don't actually like your siblings. Why, then, would you want to think of fellow Christians as brothers and sisters? Let's jump into our time machines and travel back to the ancient world to answer this vital question. Since we're talking about how the Bible defines the church, we must also ask how the biblical authors and audiences understood the sibling relationship.

Siblingship takes pride of place among the close-knit kinship bonds of the ancient family. In his book entitled *The Ancient Church as Family*, Joseph Hellerman contrasts ancient kinship group values with modern Western ideals. For example, many of us exalt the marriage relationship above all others, both in affection and loyalty. Yet, Hellerman comments, "Given a choice between 'agreement between brothers' and 'a wife and husband who live in harmony,' the ancient would choose the former hands-down."[13] Let's look at three ancient texts that illustrate the priority of the sibling relationship in the New Testament world.

First, the historian Herodotus provides an example of the sibling bond from outside the Greco-Roman world when he tells the brief story of the unnamed wife of Intaphrenes. After Darius the Great claimed the Persian throne in 522 BC, vassal nations revolted, including the Babylonians. In response, Darius commissioned a team of seven warriors to raise armies and put down the rebels. Intaphrenes went to Babylon and removed the rebel leader, regaining control for Darius. Upon his return, Intaphrenes demanded to see the king while, according to Herodotus, Darius was enjoying the company of

12. Emphasis added. Unfortunately, the NIV, NET, and NLT remove the familial language, replacing it with "believers."

13. Hellerman, *Ancient Church as Family*, 36, lists Neh 4:14; Tacitus, *Hist.* 5.8 as examples.

one of his wives. The impatient Intaphrenes maimed Darius's guards, causing the paranoid young king to arrest his former general as a traitor. Darius condemned Intaphrenes to death along with his family, except for his wife.

Darius then offered the woman a strange opportunity. She could redeem one member of her family. The grieving woman asked the king to spare her brother. When Darius asked her to explain the decision, the woman offered a pragmatic answer. Herodotus writes, "'O King,' she answered, 'another husband I may get, if heaven so will, and other children, if I lose these; but my father and mother are dead, and so I can by no means get another brother; that is why I have thus spoken.' Darius was pleased, and thought the reason good; he delivered to the woman him for whose life she had asked, and the eldest of her sons besides; all the rest he put to death."[14] I shudder to imagine having to choose between family members in a life-or-death situation. But I would put my wife and kids first without a second thought. Not so in the ancient world.

Our second text bridges the gap between sixth-century BC Persians described by Herodotus and the New Testament world. In his first-century AD treatise *On Brotherly Love*, the philosopher Plutarch comments on the wife of Intaphrenes, writing, "Rightly, then, did the Persian woman declare, when she chose to save her brother in place of her children, that she could get other children, but not another brother, since her parents were dead."[15] Plutarch's entire essay demonstrates the priority of the sibling relationship in the Greco-Roman world. Just before his comments about the Persian woman, Plutarch notes that conflict in any relationship causes pain. Conflict between brothers, though, hurts the most because of the natural intimacy of siblings. Plutarch writes about fighting brothers, "Such an enmity keeps the painful situation ever before our eyes, and reminds us every day of the madness and folly which has made the sweetest countenance of the nearest kinsman become most frowning and angry to look upon, and that voice which has been beloved and familiar from boyhood most dreadful to hear."[16] For Plutarch, the intensity of the brotherly bond makes discord between siblings the most pitiful of states. And, in case you missed it, he referred to a brother as "the nearest kinsman." Would you say the same?

A Greek-speaking Jew likely wrote our final text in the early to mid-first-century AD.[17] The book known as 4 Maccabees offers valuable insights

---

14. Herodotus, *Hist.* 3, 119 (Godley, LCL).

15. Plutarch, *Frat. amor.*, 7 (Helmbold, LCL).

16. Plutarch, *Frat. amor.*, 7 (Helmbold, LCL).

17. deSilva, "Third and Fourth Maccabees," 664. My recognition of this text's value for familial backgrounds is due to Hellerman, *Ancient Church as Family*, 42–44.

into the natural affection between siblings. The author writes, "You are not ignorant of the bonds of brotherhood, which the divine and all-wise Providence has allotted through fathers to their descendants, implanting them through their mother's womb. In that womb brothers dwell an equal length of time and are shaped for the same time. They grow from the same blood, and from the same life-spring they are brought to mature birth. . . . They grow more robust through common nurture, daily companionship, other education and our discipline in divine law. So strong, indeed, is the sympathy of brotherly love."[18] The author of 4 Maccabees attributes the strong brotherly bond to common lineage, shared childhood experiences, and concurrent growth.

These three texts demonstrate the close bond between siblings in three different ancient cultures: Persian, Greek, and Jewish. We could add stories where a wife sides with her brother when he battles her husband. We could look at the role of arranged marriages or the horrific practice of exposing unwanted children on trash heaps. But, our point remains the same. Above any other relationship, the sibling bond took pride of place in both affection and loyalty. In this cultural context, the New Testament authors leave their physical siblings behind and celebrate their spiritual brothers and sisters as their most prized relationships.

Jews vs. Gentiles

Now that we're on the same page about the ancient family, we can begin to see how pervasive the family metaphor was in the early church. As Acts 1:15 suggests, Luke begins his history of the church by calling gathered believers *the siblings*, not using the word *church* until Acts 5:11. Familial language was a carryover from Judaism. The book of Acts reveals that Jews (whether they believe in Jesus or not) commonly called each other siblings, since Father Abraham had many sons and many sons had Father Abraham. But, the real shock comes in Acts, when Jewish Christians begin to see non-Jewish Christians as siblings.

Remember, the divide between Jews and non-Jews was more of a canyon than a ditch. Jews lived by strict moral and cultural laws that governed what they ate and wore, with whom they associated, and what sexual practices were acceptable. The Law of Moses defined purity and holiness for God's chosen people. Later, the exile showed that God was serious about it. Gentiles (a somewhat derogatory term for non-Jews) lived by a different standard. To the Jews, gentiles were like Charlie Brown's friend Pigpen.

18. Fourth Macc 13:19–23a NETS.

Filthiness seemed to waft off of them as they walked by. If their paganism were not hard enough to stomach, their dietary and sexual practices would cause even the sturdiest Jew to gag. Imagine attending a church fellowship meal with a new Christian who brought a baked puppy to share and whose dinner conversation consisted of outlining his sexual conquests. And now you can feel some sympathy for early Jewish Christians.

Due to their general revulsion toward gentiles, we can hardly blame Jewish Christians for their passionate misunderstanding. Gentiles who wished to follow Jesus must first obey what God already commanded in the Old Testament, right? In essence, they thought potential gentile converts needed to become Jews before they believed in Jesus. After two millennia of studying Paul's letters, we have a hard time accepting that any Christian would deny salvation through Christ alone apart from works of the law (see Rom 3:21–26). But from their perspective, early Jewish believers were simply trying to be faithful to God. And wouldn't it be better if every believer were on the same page about what to eat and how to act? Wouldn't uniformity bring unity to the church?

The storm of questions and concerns finally arrived in Jerusalem in Acts 15 as the earliest (Jewish) church leaders gathered to determine the fate of gentile converts. Their fascinating discussion is worth reading, but more important for our purposes is the striking language of the greeting sent to gentile believers. "And they sent this letter by them, 'The apostles and the brethren who are elders, *to the brethren* in Antioch and Syria and Cilicia *who are from the Gentiles*, greetings'" (Acts 15:23 NASB, emphasis added). Now, because of the gospel, Jewish believers addressed gentile believers as siblings. How incredible that gentile Christians aren't merely fellow believers or church members but are brothers and sisters—family! The term *siblings* occurs ten times in Acts 15 alone (compared to only four occurrences of the word *church*). And throughout the rest of the New Testament, *siblings* becomes the preferred term for a gathering of believers.

Paul and the other New Testament authors continued writing about the church using familial language. Sibling terminology is not a New Testament nicety. It reveals the unseen foundation of all the church would become. The church is a family, and when believers begin to live like it, everything falls into place: the church's purpose, the pastor's role, the relationship between church members, and more.

SWAPPING METAPHORS: EVALUATE
YOUR PARADIGM

Since the New Testament prioritizes family language over any other way of speaking about the church, the first question to ask is, "Do I?" How do you view what the church *is*? Keep in mind that the two metaphors—"The church is a business" and "The church is a family"—are not the only possible paradigms. You might see the church as a social club, school, political rally, therapy center, or any other number of root metaphors. So, the first question is, "How do you see the church?" And the second is, "Why do you see it that way?"

Shaping Our Roots

We must become aware of our root metaphors and evaluate them. I believe that the pervasive corporate-church model has deceptively dangerous implications for church life. So whether you are a church leader or member, consider the implications of your root metaphor. Let me offer some questions that small group leaders or a church staff may use to get the conversation rolling:

- How does your root metaphor impact what you think the church should do?

- How might it impact your perspective on church membership, the worship service, giving, classes and small groups, staffing, or your role as part of a church?

- What do you consider success and failure in the church?

- Is there a biblical foundation for your concept of the church?

Beyond considering the implications of our root metaphors, we must evaluate influencers who shape our understanding of the church. The number of books, blogs, and podcasts on church leadership is too large to count. We live in the information age, where you can find multiple answers to nearly any question you might ask, but we must be wary of the answers we hear. Not every solution we find builds upon a biblical foundation for church life. Even worse, some authors and speakers may not be aware of their root metaphors. They dispense buckets of advice without considering the source of the spring from which they draw. So, it is up to you to listen closely for the paradigms guiding your favorite church leadership gurus. If their paradigm is bad, you should approach their wisdom with caution.

Regulating Our Consumption

Most of us worry little about our safety. We buy groceries at the store and never ask if our food is safe to eat. Take chocolate, for example. The cocoa bean comes from a fruit (so, chocolate is a fruit, right?) and goes through quite a process before reaching your mouth.[19] Along the way, there are several opportunities for the cocoa product to come into contact with, let's say, less-than-appetizing substances. One concern of the FDA is what they label as "mammalian excreta," also known as animal feces. No one wants to drink that kind of flavored hot chocolate, so we have the FDA to help protect us. They allow only ten milligrams of excrement per pound of cocoa. Before you toss your Hersheys, keep in mind that ten milligrams equal about 0.0002 percent of feces in a pound of cocoa. By comparison, they allow forty-five rodent hairs (and over thirteen-hundred "insect fragments") in a pound of ground allspice.[20] You're welcome.

My point is that a government agency regulates what we consume to protect us from illness. But when it comes to what we ingest as readers and listeners, there is no FDA, especially for blogs and podcasts (books at least have publishers). Thankfully, we don't need a "Food Defect Levels Handbook" like the FDA publishes for its employees. We have the word of God. And close readers will exalt biblical paradigms to filter out all of the corporate-church "rodent hair," and the church will be better for it.

As we confront the prevailing root metaphor of the day, that the church is a business, we will discover how entrenched it is. Like a vine that grows to fill every nook and notch outside a home, you may find the corporate-church metaphor hidden everywhere within your view of the church. Still, the task's difficulty must not stop us from doing the hard work of removing what is unhealthy from our hearts and our churches. Believers (and non-believers) are searching for something more than another business or club; they're searching for a family. And God has graciously provided a family for believers, if only we will lovingly prune our view of the church.

19. "Where Does Chocolate Come From?"
20. FDA, "Food Defect Levels Handbook."

3

The Group First, Not the Individual

The Background of Siblingship in the Early Church

Remember, you're the only one who matters. You are the only person who knows what's best for you. . . . Always, always listen to yourself and what you want first.

—STEPHENIE ZAMORA

AT THE TURN OF the millennium, I embarked on my first youth mission trip to Houston, Texas. My youth pastor, Doug Bischoff, wisely insisted the team meet beforehand to prepare a Vacation Bible School for a struggling Houston community. At our meeting, I discovered that none of my close friends were going to Houston. I was surrounded by older, established youth group members, and I was terrified to leave home for ten days as an outsider. It was a teenager's worst nightmare. The dangerous conditions we would face in Houston didn't concern me. I could handle twelve hours in a church van and could sleep on a half-inflated air mattress on a dirty gymnasium floor. But, the possibility of isolation was frightening for a soon-to-be high school freshman who had been the new kid at school three times in the last five years. If I had thought my parents would let me, I would have quit the trip.

Two decades later, I can still remember three rules that Doug instilled in us during our training. First, he banned the word *hot* from our vocabulary. Yes, we were going to Houston in mid-July, but what good would complaining do? In practice, we found creative ways to complain by expanding our vocabularies (warm, steamy, toasty, oppressive, etc.).

The second rule was also straightforward: be flexible. The type As among us must not fossilize their plans because missions work requires adaptation. If our host church needed us to clean a bathroom, we would grab the Comet and toilet brush. If our dinner or shower time changed, we would remain hungry and stinky a while longer. The big idea was that the trip was not about us—not our comfort or personal benefit.

The third rule was a prohibition. Doug allowed no phones, video game systems, or Discmans on the trip (for younger readers, Discmans were clunky, portable devices that played these little discs called CDs). Keep in mind that the year was 2000. Most of us didn't own a cell phone, and the lucky few who did mainly used them to make calls, believe it or not. Even texting someone once cost ten cents. Still, all distractions had to stay at home. Doug wanted to rid our lives of the garbage we so often ingested, at least for those ten days, and the result was profound. A dozen teenagers prepared to teach impoverished children about Jesus in an environment where complaining was limited, flexible attitudes replaced self-centered thinking, and we had nothing better to do than talk with each other. It's no surprise that when I returned home after ten days in Houston, a new family came with me.

The Houston trip provided a valuable lesson: those who believe in Jesus won't act like family by accident. Just as newlyweds who wish to grow a healthy marriage must do so purposefully, so also must our churches create intentional family growth opportunities. My youth pastor deliberately eliminated the sources of bad attitudes and personal barriers, and, as a result, God grew a group of gangly teenagers into a community. But what happens when we let our guard down and unintentionally communicate that the church is a business? In other words, what is the baseline, the typical worldview that will drive our churches if we don't grab the wheel? If American history is any indication, individualism will occupy the driver's seat.

IF THE CHURCH IS A BUSINESS, IT'S ALL ABOUT ME

Sociologists recognize that there are two basic approaches to society: individualistic or collectivistic. The founding fathers built the United States of America as an individualistic nation, meaning that individual rights, liberties, goals, and values were most important. Simply put, I do what *I* want, not what *they* want me to do. The recipe for American individualism began with two essential ingredients.[1]

The Ingredients of Individualism

First, the Protestant Reformation emphasized the personal nature of faith over the authority of a group of priests. When Martin Luther nailed his ninety-five theses to the church door, he didn't intend to create a social revolution. Yet, Luther pulled Scripture out of the hands of priests and put it into the hands of the people, fundamentally changing Christianity. Reforming a world religion also altered the societies of the newly Reformed Christians. The Protestant movement Luther planted eventually yielded an individualistic approach to faith, the fruit of which was personal freedom of worship and individual spiritual disciplines. The colonists who flooded what would become the United States brought their personal faith and individualistic worldview, providing a critical ingredient to what would become modern Evangelicalism.

The second ingredient was the philosophy of John Locke. Locke wrote influential works that shaped America as we know it, especially his *Two Treatises of Government*, published in 1689. Locke believed that while society and government matter, the individual takes precedence, not the group.[2] Stay with me, because this subtle distinction is important. Locke wanted the government to work for the people, not the people for the government. Thanks to the Reformation and the career of John Locke, I am not firstly an American citizen (nor a Missourian or a Kimbrough). I'm me. I don't identify myself by my group, and my priority is not what will help my group(s) prosper but what will benefit me. Such is the norm today in the Western world.

The founders' individualistic spirit continues to impact every realm of American culture. A few years ago, Burger King altered its forty-year-old slogan "Have it your way" to "Be your way." The new motto is no longer a statement about food but a philosophy of life. A Burger King spokesperson described the new slogan this way: "[People] can and should live how they want anytime. It's OK to not be perfect . . . . Self-expression is most important and it's our differences that make us individuals instead of robots."[3] I'm not sure what authorizes a fast-food chain to pontificate about how people should live, but BK's answer exposes our individualistic ideals. Life coach

1. Davenport and Lloyd, *Rugged Individualism*, 6–11.
2. Davenport and Lloyd, *Rugged Individualism*, 9.
3. Associated Press, "Burger King Ditches."

Stephenie Zamora is a less surprising spokesperson for individualism. She advises, "Remember, you're the only one who matters. You are the only person who knows what's best for you. . . . Always, always listen to yourself and what you want first."[4] The heart and soul of the individualistic worldview are that I come first. My dreams and desires matter more than those of my group. Family, town, and nation are all secondary, and I shouldn't feel guilty about it.

My intention is not to argue for or against individualism at the government or even societal levels. Also, it would be misleading to act as if there were no collectivist spirit in America, especially in politics. Yet, the individualistic ideal is dominant today. Nearly every movie, TV show, and novel tells us "Be yourself" and "Don't let anyone tell you what to do!" For example, the ice queen Elsa sings one of the most iconic Disney songs of the last few decades, "Let It Go." Elsa's parents force her to hide her true self after an icy blast injures her sister. But Elsa longs for the apparently higher good of freedom from accountability, freedom to do what she alone desires, and freedom from interacting with anyone else, all of which she expresses in the chorus of "Let It Go." Elsa rejects the need to do what is best for her family or kingdom, choosing instead to break out on her own—to be an individual, free from the chains of society's expectations. Even though Elsa's closed-off lifestyle acts as the antagonist of the movie—putting her sister and her people at risk—kids and adults together sing "Let It Go" as a celebration of authentic, individualistic freedom.

If you're a Westerner like me, you may be struggling right now to guess what the problem is. You've likely known only individualism. Maybe you can't even imagine how a society could operate differently. But, throughout most of human history, collectivist (or group-first) cultures have dominated. The collectivist mentality "encourages conformity and discourages individuals from dissenting and standing out."[5] Anthropologist Bruce Malina describes group-first systems this way: "The individual person is embedded in the group and is free to do what he or she feels right and necessary only if in accord with group norms and only if the action is in the group's best interest."[6] If a young man wants to leave his family and village behind, his group-first society will shame him verbally and physically with hopes of bringing the man back into obedience to the group. Arranged marriages are also common in group-first cultures. By marrying my son to a potential business partner's daughter, I can increase my family's status. It doesn't

4. Zamora, "How to Handle Life."

5. Gorodnichenko and Roland, "Understanding Individualism-Collectivism Cleavage," 2.

6. Malina, *Christian Origins*, 19.

matter if my son is in love or not. He'll do what's best for the family. So, it isn't that collectivist societies have no sense of the individual, but the individual's value and identity derive from the group's identity. When the family or village prospers, the individual prospers. When an individual embarrasses himself, he embarrasses the group, too.

The Scent of Individualism

Now that the distinctions between collectivistic and individualistic societies are clear, let's return to our present situation. America is individualistic, so those of us who are Americans tend to think in individualistic terms. We don't mean to prioritize the individual, yet to do so seems normal to us. We bear the scent of individualism.

Emily and I bought a 112-year-old house when we got married. The house was built in 1897 and had unique features like some ornate, original doorknobs and a creepy dirt-floor basement that flooded every time it rained. Although our neighborhood was run down, we had kind neighbors like Randy and Mary, who often caught our dog when he ran away. Randy and Mary had a soft spot for the neighborhood animals, and they would leave bowls of food and water out for all of the strays in the areas: dogs, cats, and (unintentionally, I'm sure) skunks.

One November, Emily and I left to visit my best friend in Nashville for the weekend. When we came home, we discovered that a terrorist skunk had bombed our house. The smell was almost painful, and every nook and cranny of our house reeked. Couch cushions? Reeked. Silverware? Stank. Every item of clothing we owned? Nearly unsalvageable. We had to leave our windows open (in November, remember) for days and had to wash anything and everything we could. I imagine we also single-handedly paid the salary that year of the CEO of Febreze. It was so bad—and this is true—that people would give us clothes to change into at work because they didn't want to smell us. The most frustrating part was discovering months and years later that the stench clung to items I didn't think to clean. For a long time, I kept noticing my hands smelled skunky when I got to work. Can you guess what the problem was? I hadn't thought to wash my car keys or my belt. My acoustic guitar continues to exude the odor of skunk sometimes. And to this day, the smell of skunk gives me anxiety.

Once we got our house back in order, my first mission was to prevent a second attack. After some brilliant detective work, I determined the skunk had crawled under one of our porches, dug a hole that led underneath the house, and taken up residence just below the hundred-year-old hardwood floor (with no subfloor) in our living room closet. The skunk was gone, of course, when I made this discovery, so I used his absence to block the holes with cinder blocks, surround the porch with rags soaked in ammonia, and so on. I'd like to say the story had a happy ending—that the skunk repented and made restitution—but, instead, he launched counterattacks several times before we moved a few years later.

I'm sure the analogy is clear, but let me spell it out nonetheless. The cultural norm of individualism is like a powerful, pervasive smell that clings to everything in its vicinity. Your job will smell like it. Your marriage, exercise class, and favorite movies carry its scent. Even your church cannot escape the individualistic odor that surrounds it. The only difference is that, unlike the skunk, you don't recognize the perfume because you've become accustomed to it. Consequently, the aroma of individualism is even harder to scrub away from places it shouldn't be because we don't smell it anymore.

Me, Myself, and I

Our worship music is one place where the scent of individualism is strong (for those with a nose to smell it). I led a contemporary worship band for fifteen years and only recently realized that most of our songs use first-person singular pronouns: *I, me, my*. Plural pronouns like *we, us,* and *our* are few and far between. As I write, the most popular worship song, according to CCLI, is "Reckless Love."[7] The song latches on to a seemingly individualistic parable about a shepherd who leaves ninety-nine sheep searching for the lost one.

Jesus's parable in Luke 15 emphasizes God's great love for the sinner, much like the adjacent parable of the prodigal son. The story's point is that the shepherd will not react in anger or seek to punish the lost sheep but instead continues to pursue it and rejoices when he rescues it. The shepherd leaves the ninety-nine because they are safe, not because he cares only about the lone sheep. In addition, the shepherd's response reveals the collectivist mindset of the first century: "And when he comes home, he calls together his friends and his neighbors, saying to them, 'Rejoice with me, for I have found my sheep which was lost!'" (Luke 15:6 NASB). The happy shepherd doesn't celebrate by buying himself a pizza and binge-watching Netflix alone but by rejoicing with his community—his friends and neighbors.

My point is that the Bible records Jesus's parable in a way that doesn't carry the scent of individualism, but our modern worship lyrics can't escape

7. Christian Copyright Licensing International, https://us.ccli.com/, accessed May 31, 2019.

the odor. Whether you think the description of God's love as *reckless* is theologically fair game or not (and words do matter!), the number one worship song reveals that individualistic thinking is typical in today's church. The song includes no reference to *us*—the church—or to God's love for anyone but *me*.

"Reckless Love" is not alone in this trend, nor is the trend new. Worship researchers Segler and Bradley blame the Puritans for normalizing individualistic lyrics, writing, "Puritanism carried individualism and subjectivity to the extreme. The concept of the church at worship as a corporate unit was practically lost. The Puritan congregation was a collection of individuals at prayer; the service was more concerned with the individual than the corporate body."[8] We could also look to the famous eighteenth-century hymn "Amazing Grace," which moves beyond *me* only in the later-added final stanza, "When *we've* been there . . ." The truth is, the vast majority of worship songs written in the last three hundred years reveal an individualistic orientation. I rejoice that their lyrics exalt Christ and glorify God, but their background harmonies quietly sing, "It's all about me."

As we mentioned earlier, both the Reformation and Enlightenment philosophy fed the individualistic spirit that prevails today. But the father of the Reformation, Martin Luther, famously published songs that addressed believers corporately. Consider lyrics from his "Lord, Keep Us Steadfast in Thy Word":

> Lord Jesus Christ, Your pow'r make known,
> For you are Lord of lords alone;
> Defend Your *holy Church*, that *we*
> May sing your praise triumphantly.[9]

The most famous of Luther's hymns also sounds collectivistic, at least in its view of the church. The lyrics read:

> A mighty fortress is *our* God,
> A bulwark never failing;
> *Our* helper he, amid the flood
> Of mortal ills prevailing.
> For still *our* ancient foe
> Doth seek to work *us* woe;
> His craft and pow'r are great,
> And, armed with cruel hate

---

8. Segler and Bradley, *Christian Worship*, 38.
9. Luther, "Lord, Keep Us Steadfast" (emphasis added).

On earth is not his equal.[10]

Songs even older than Luther's, such as the thirteenth-century hymn "All Creatures of Our God and King," confirm that group-first thinking was once the norm for Christian worship lyrics. Unfortunately, the church has found itself swept along by a river of cultural norms, and only a strong pair of legs and a heart of determination can return us safely to the shore.

The Corporate-Church Crisis and Individualism

The corporate-church model is not to blame for this crisis, since it came along after our individualistic patterns were firmly established. Isn't, then, the business approach as viable as any other? Well, if our goal is to maintain the status quo, then all hail the business model. Modern American businesses feed on individualism. Consider, for example, the role of individuality in our increasing push for customization. How do you want your hamburger cooked? Do you want the black, silver, white, coral, magenta, or sunset phone cover? What is your ideal delivery time? Would you like to substitute another side? The business world says I'm an individual, and I should have it my way. A cookie-cutter product would melt the unique snowflake that is my individuality. So, the business model will suffice if we are content with a customization-driven, customer-focused, me-centered view of the church.

The individualistic focus of the corporate-church model produces a variety of results. Believers see themselves as mere consumers with no attachment to their current church product (more on this in a later chapter). Pastors feel pressure to focus more on what is trending in their communities than on implementing biblical principles in their current contexts. Churches willingly fracture themselves into ministry silos, so that each demographic can get the music they like and the teaching style they prefer. I can't even keep track of the worship styles anymore: traditional, contemporary, blended, legacy, liturgical, or hair-band. Okay, I made the last one up, but would it surprise anyone?

The most frightening outcome of the individualistic approach to church life is that believers simply don't care about each other. No one notices the single dad whose most significant victory is getting his kids clothed, fed, and in the church building. We're too focused on ourselves. We feel bad that a middle-aged church member was diagnosed with Parkinson's, but we sense no obligation to care for her as she deteriorates. We leave the dozens

---

10. Luther, "A Mighty Fortress," stanza 1 (emphasis added).

of couples contemplating divorce on an island. Lonely seniors are outside our field of vision. Yes, the corporate church asks its members to love one another, even creating programs to facilitate deep affection. But, every other part of church life shouts from the steeple, "It's all about you! Have it your way!" So, the noise of individualism drowns out our appeals to find biblical community.

The corporate church will struggle to go round after round against the barrage of cultural norms. Businesses thrive when they submit to society's passions and priorities. For example, trendsetters now inform us that the stylish among us must decorate our homes with natural wooden accents, so even Walmart is cluttered with rustic wooden picture frames and wall décor destined to give splinters to interior designers. If you're a salesperson, it pays to be in the know—to give the people what they want. But should a church follow when society leads?

The Bible does not take a stand on every cultural issue, but God has always called his people to countercultural living in ways meant to preserve their identity in him and focus their worship on him. So, is individualism permissible among God's people today, or does the New Testament draw up a blueprint for a group-first church? In other words, can individualistic values and biblical norms for the church coexist?

IF THE CHURCH IS A FAMILY, THE GROUP TAKES PRIORITY

The world of the Bible is collectivistic. The family comes first, not the individual. And every person has a role to play.

Collectivism Explained

If young Joe fled his family's leather business and struck out on his own, he left behind a gaping hole that would wound his family. Or, imagine that Joe was the only son of his father, the town leatherworker. Like most men in the New Testament era, Joe's father was unlikely to live past forty years old. If Joe chose to pursue his dreams in the big city, he would leave his mother and youngest sisters without a breadwinner and his town without a leatherworker. You might be thinking that these expectations aren't fair, that the group put too much pressure on Joe. But, first-century families did not think this way. God had placed Joe in his family in a particular town for the benefit of others. Joe didn't choose where he was born, and he would never dream of sacrificing everyone else by traveling his own path.

Collectivist values are difficult to grasp for most of us. We find ancient naming practices silly and archaic because we would never identify ourselves by our fathers.[11] We're a first-name kind of society, so I don't refer to myself as Matt, son of Max, son of Don. Doing so would cause people to doubt my sanity. And we certainly don't add our hometowns to our names, like Mary from Magdala (Mary Magdalene). More importantly, the group is not our primary source of identity, and we don't base our decisions on the group's best interests. You may be proud to be an American, but you want to pay as little in taxes as legally possible, even though you know taxes help the nation. Maybe you hated the rival high school when you were a student, but if that special someone attended the enemy school, you probably didn't feel any qualms about pursuing your crush. If this mirrors your experience, I have a reality check for you: none of your biblical heroes would have thought like you.

Just because the New Testament authors wrote when collectivism ruled the day does not automatically mean the church should operate with a group-first mindset. We're all products of our culture. Thus, we must ask if the New Testament explicitly teaches that the church must function as a collectivist island in the middle of its cultural stream. Put another way, is individualism biblically permissible? In *When the Church Was a Family*, Joseph Hellerman answers these questions, writing, "The collectivist social model is deeply woven into the very fabric of the gospel itself."[12] We'll talk more in the next chapter about the gospel core of the church-family model, but for now, let's look at one example of a group-first, familial approach to church life.

The Situation in Corinth

First Corinthians 8–10 depicts a fascinating struggle in the early church revolving around food. As strange as it may seem, food problems pop up in the Gospels, Acts, Romans 14, again in 1 Corinthians 11, Galatians 2, and elsewhere. The problem was twofold: with whom could they share a table, and what could they eat? The *with whom* question was a Jewish problem, since they believed that non-Jews made everything unclean. Even to sit at the table with a non-Jew made the Jew impure. For Paul, though, the gospel of Jesus Christ overcame this particular ethnic distinction and, even more,

11. Hellerman, *When Church Was Family*, 21–22.
12. Hellerman, *When Church Was Family*, 31.

required believing Jews and Gentiles to dine together (see Gal 2). Ancient fellowship suppers demonstrated the unity the gospel demanded.

While the *with whom* problem had a straightforward answer, the issue of *what* to eat was more nuanced. Was any food out of bounds for the church? Do Christians live under any food laws? The Old Testament provided a law code that directed Israel to eat only certain foods, eliminating pork and shellfish, for example. Bacon-wrapped shrimp was off the table. God wanted to set his people apart, and a regulated diet was part of Israel's uniqueness. By the New Testament era, the Jewish people had avoided such foods for over a thousand years. That's quite a habit to break.

In answer to what believers can eat, God shows Peter a magic carpet with clean and unclean animals intermingling (Acts 10:9–16). In the vision, God tells Peter to eat, but the typically brash disciple-turned-apostle refuses. "But Peter said, 'By no means, Lord, for I have never eaten anything unholy and unclean.' Again a voice came to him a second time, 'What God has cleansed, no longer consider unholy'" (Acts 10:14–15 NASB). We may think Peter is crazy to reject the glory of a well-cooked pork chop, but think how you would feel if God told you to eat dogs, cats, or stink bugs (all of which people in other parts of the world eat). Acts 10 would have offended Jewish sensibilities, but the message was clear for the young church. Peter should no longer worry about the impurity of certain foods, and by extension, food should not keep believers apart.

With Peter's vision in mind, we come to 1 Corinthians 8–10 and the issue of meat sacrificed to idols. The city of Corinth was filled with pagan temples, as were most cities of the day. People visited temples not only to appease their gods but also to hire prostitutes and have a good meal. As strange as it may sound, pagans could worship idols, have sex, and eat out at the local temple. Temples provided a buffet of temptations.

Paul came to Corinth to proclaim the gospel to people whose everyday lives included visiting temples. Consequently, those who believed in Jesus had some lifestyle changes to work out. Paul warned that idol worship and faith in Jesus could not mix. One temple activity was out the window. The Corinthians continued to struggle with sexual temptation (see 1 Cor 5–7), but presumably, Paul introduced Christian sexual ethics quickly after conversion. The apostle had now outlawed two-thirds of their former temple activities, but what about the final: eating temple food? Let's turn to 1 Corinthains 8 and consider the beginning of Paul's response.

To Meat or Not to Meat

Paul begins in verses 1–6 with knowledge. Some know-it-alls in the church thought they could win an argument through sheer brilliance. Some theologically sophisticated believers arrogantly argued with an uneducated group about the nature of the gods. Were Zeus, Apollo, Artemis, and Athena real gods or not? Was the believer participating in the worship of an actual deity when he ate meat sacrificed to a god? If not, wasn't idol meat acceptable? Paul admits that only one God exists, and believers do not commune with any real god when enjoying a side of lamb from the local temple. We would expect, then, for Paul to close the issue with a simple command, such as "so, eat whatever you want." But he goes on.

In verse 7, Paul acknowledges church members who have weak consciences and cannot accept that idol meat carries no religious meaning. You can hear the arrogant group saying, "But you know Poseidon, Hera, and Ares aren't real gods! What is your problem? Get it through your heads, and stop worrying about your steak." Their view of God is accurate, so I would expect Paul to agree with their conclusion. But, actually, all of Paul's comments seem to urge avoiding idol meat. First, eating idol meat will not draw the Corinthians closer to God. Second, avoiding idol meat won't harm anyone. Third, those who eat meat sacrificed to idols gain no advantage from it. These statements cause some scholars to conclude that Paul is morally opposed to the practice of eating idol meat, except when a believer doesn't know what he's eating.[13] However, verse 9 clears the waters, in my opinion. Paul refers to eating idol meat as "your liberty" and then offers instructions on using Christian freedom rightly. So, while Paul may prefer that his converts avoid idol meat altogether, he does not believe he has the theological right to prohibit it. Instead, he warns the "knowledge group" that they must not trip up weak consciences.

Paul clarifies in verse 10 what a stumbling block would look like. "For if someone sees you, who have knowledge, dining in an idol's temple, will not his conscience, if he is weak, be strengthened to eat things sacrificed to idols?" Paul does not warn the idol-meat-eaters that they might offend or bug another believer by exercising their freedoms. Feelings of annoyance are not Paul's concern. The apostle wants to prevent weak Christians from engaging in activities they believe are sinful.

Paul envisions that a weak new convert, Julia, sees her Christian friend, Julius, eating at the temple of Artemis. Julia's conscience won't let her eat at the temple, but she respects her friend so much that she decides

---

13. Cheung, *Idol Food in Corinth*, 296–99; Garland, "Dispute over Food Sacrificed."

to indulge. She joins Julius for lunch, all the while sweating nervously and feeling a bit sick to her stomach. Afterward, Julia returns home filled with regret, begins to doubt her faith, and eventually gives up on her commitments to Christ. This situation was such a threat that Paul devoted several chapters to the issue.

Appealing to Family

At this point in the argument, Paul introduces sibling language. Paul uses familial terminology throughout 1 Corinthians, but nowhere is it more concentrated than in 8:11–13. But why not call them believers, beloved, or elect? Why does Paul seem to emphasize siblingship? Paul's instructions depend on a sense of love and mutual concern within the church. If Paul's converts identified themselves foremost as co-workers or fellow citizens of heaven, then he would have no basis upon which to build his guidelines. Church members would be loosely connected people who all happened to believe in Jesus. But, if Paul could help the Corinthians see that they were now a diverse family—a committed, unified, affectionate, group-first family—then concerns over personal freedoms would fall away. Paul writes, "For through your knowledge he who is weak is ruined, the *brother* for whose sake Christ died. And so, by sinning against the *brethren* and wounding their conscience when it is weak, you sin against Christ. Therefore, if food causes my *brother* to stumble, I will never eat meat again, so that I will not cause my *brother* to stumble" (1 Cor 8:11–13 NASB, emphasis added).

The last thing a sibling would want to do in the family-centered world of ancient Corinth is to ruin (v. 11), sin against (v. 12a), wound (v. 12b), or trip up a brother or sister (v. 13). Plutarch penned an entire essay on sibling relationships, revealing attitudes that the Corinthians likely shared. Not long after Paul's lifetime, the Greek philosopher Plutarch wrote, "Brothers should not be like the scales of a balance, the one rising upon the other's sinking; but rather like numbers in arithmetic, the lesser and greater mutually helping and improving each other."[14] While our culture would argue that my freedom comes first, and I am not my brother's keeper (see Gen 3), the ancient world would have disagreed. You are responsible for the well-being of your siblings because the group comes first. Paul's only need, then, was to convince Corinthian believers that the church was now their family.

As Paul's argument in 1 Corinthians 8 progresses, he points them to the death of Christ (v. 11). Those who sin against the family (NASB, *the brethren*) also sin against Christ (v. 12). If the liberty of those with knowledge

14. Plutarch, *Frat. amor.*, 15 (Goodwin).

causes their siblings to betray their consciences, then liberty has become sinful. Consider what happened at a San Antonio Spurs basketball game in January 2017. Kawhi Leonard stole the ball from his teammate, Pau Gasol, who was looking to pass to an open player. Leonard ran behind Gasol and snatched the ball, apparently thinking he could make the play. Although Leonard scored, he embarrassed himself, his team, and the city of San Antonio. Leonard's overzealousness reflected poorly on everyone because he represented his group. Believers might not share a team name or live in the same location. For us, Jesus is the family trait that links Christian siblings together. Our actions reflect on one another because we're a family.

The Individual for the Group

In all, 1 Corinthians 8 demonstrates the practical benefit of seeing the church as a family. Unlike the individualistic business model of church life, the church family can overcome conflict among believers. First, the family model promotes strong-group values, where the individual member pursues what is best for the family. Collectivism does not praise individuals who forsake or wound their siblings, whether in the name of liberty or to pursue their own dreams. Honorable siblings do what is best for the family. Paul's view of the church builds upon these values, even labeling the rejection of strong-group ideals as sin. In the church, the family comes first.

The second foundation for Paul's exhortation in 1 Corinthians 8 is the siblingship of believers in Christ. The corporate-church model of church life has no basis to require commitment and affection between members. Fellow shoppers don't love or pursue what is best for one another. But ancient families lived together, ate together, worked together, succeeded or failed together, and worshiped together. If one member suffered, the group bore the responsibility to care for him. If someone injured a sister, the family would correct him and reconcile the two. Members who had more would help those who had less. Family carried a lifetime commitment. And Paul urged the church he planted to see itself as a family.

SWAPPING METAPHORS: PUTTING INDIVIDUALISM IN ITS PLACE

For those of us who swim in the sea of Western individualism, collectivism seems an archaic way of life. Joseph Hellerman will help us begin to navigate the implications of a group-first view of church life. He writes, "I am hardly naïve enough to suggest that modern Americans ought to return to the extended family systems of generations ago. We hold on tenaciously to our hard-won personal freedoms. But we must recognize that we have paid a tremendous emotional and spiritual price to be released from the cultural shackles reflected in the [group-first] values of our ancestors."[15] Hellerman is right that we should not scrap the positive results of individualism like the Bill of Rights or free speech. I would add that I am not calling for a revolution at the governmental or cultural levels. Those are subject matters for other thinkers. My only concerns are how you and I view what the church is and how we relate to fellow believers.

Identifying Individualism

As we process the practical implications of this chapter, let's start with you (irony intended). What actions and attitudes reveal your individualistic sensibilities? With a bow to Jeff Foxworthy, let's play a game to identify if you're an individualist. You might be an individualist if your independent streak causes you to pull a muscle trying to move that couch by yourself rather than ask for help. You might be an individualist if you've ever said (or thought), "I'm looking out for number one." If you've ever been annoyed that a family member told you cloth diapers would be better for your baby, you might be an individualist. You might be an individualist if you desperately pray before church that you can come and go without anyone talking to you. Truthfully, you might be an individualist if you're always first in line, if you find yourself being served but never serving, if any minor inconvenience can keep you from gathering with other believers, or if you don't care when a church member stops showing up. If you hide your deepest, darkest fears from your small group, you might be an individualist. All of us who have grown up in the West have individualistic tendencies, so I challenge you to examine your concept of church and your interaction with other believers to see where individualism has crept in and muddied the New Testament vision of church life.

Let's ask some diagnostic questions about our churches. If you are not a pastor or church leader, please show extra grace to those who are as you consider these questions. What examples of customization or other business-oriented values shape your church? Few of our churches are daring enough to hold drive-through prayer meetings or customizable Bible studies for every individual member. Still, the message of individualism is

---

15. Hellerman, *When Church Was Family*, 5.

written all over our ministries.[16] Consider your church's Bible study classes or small group ministry. Is each group so diverse that it is impossible to identify by demographic, or do you have groups customized for singles, seniors, women, retirees, young marrieds, athletes, hipsters, and redheads? Do you differentiate worship services by musical style, so that each generation can worship how they like? Does your church mind if you don't contribute? My daughter began feeding the dog as a daily chore when she was five years old. She contributed to the family as soon as she was able. Does your church urge you to help the family in some manner?

I fear we have made most church members professional spectators because we have positioned the worship service as the center of church life. The service has an important role, but shaping the church into a family is not one of them.[17] One of the few glimpses in the New Testament of a gathering of believers shows all members participating. Paul writes, "What then, *brothers and sisters*? Whenever you come together, each one has a hymn, a teaching, a revelation, another tongue, or an interpretation. Everything is to be done for building up" (1 Cor 14:26 CSB, emphasis added). When *church* consists of a weekly Sunday morning performance with a live studio audience, believers are unlikely to become a family. We need to watch how we talk about going to church (i.e., the worship service) to avoid the impression that watching and listening are all that church involvement is. We must also consider the online options we provide in order to make church accessible to non-churchgoers, admitting that even when these methods have positive ends, they can create unintended side effects. Group prayer, personal encouragement, and confession are tough to practice in a large auditorium or online.

Idol Meat Today

In addition to exposing individualism in our churches, we would be foolish to walk through 1 Corinthians 8 without asking what idol meat we might find today. Stumbling blocks are distinct to each family, but I can offer an example to get you thinking. The ministry I lead at Springhill includes several single people. Because singleness is taboo in many evangelical churches, we

16. I want to again stress that while I am not picking on larger churches, the freedom that big budgets and large member bases provide allows megachurch pastors the opportunity to customize their churches in ways small-church pastors cannot.

17. Worship services allow pastors to shape the doctrinal life of the congregation as a whole, providing a theological standard for smaller gatherings. Services also provide a glimpse of the heavenly gathering that will characterize eternity, making times of corporate worship a promise of what is to come.

regularly discuss 1 Corinthians 7, where Paul writes that singleness is a gift and a calling. Thankfully, some of our singles have acknowledged that God may have called them to an unmarried life devoted to him. Their biblically informed consciences now tell them not to treat marriage as the ultimate goal in life. But divinely ordained matchmakers don't get it. With kind intentions, they pester the single person to give that attractive new person a shot. They wear expressions of pity and focus their help on the apparent black hole in the single person's sense of joy. So the single person, after battling his conscience for a while, eventually betrays it and engages in a dating lifestyle that God has not designed for him.

In this scenario, the matchmaker causes a weaker brother to stumble. The single man betrays his God-given conscience due to pressure from a fellow believer. Dating may not be a conscience issue in your local church, but other stumbling blocks exist. You can identify them by asking where your sense of right and wrong differs from other believers. Is there an activity that the Bible does not prohibit and that raises no alarms in your heart but that another believer might consider sinful? Do you view an action with Christian freedom that someone else rejects as wrong?

I know Christians who wear suits and dresses to church every Sunday, though most Springhill members show up in jeans. Some feel convicted to eat healthy foods, and others live on fried chicken and ice cream. I believe there are biblical principles and passages that speak to all of these issues, but we see no "Thou shalt not have high cholesterol!" And instead of issuing a new law for every foreseeable point of contention, Paul demands a spirit of selfless sacrifice. He concludes in 1 Corinthians 8:13 (NASB), "Therefore, if food causes my brother to stumble, I will never eat meat again, so that I will not cause my brother to stumble." Your obligation, then, is to be proactive, protecting your siblings at all costs. In a group-first family like the church, you should readily give up personal freedoms if doing so helps your group. The family comes first. And in case you're wondering, the more mature Christians will sacrifice much more than the spiritual babies. This is the way of the cross.

Leading the Group

Those of us who are pastors and ministry leaders bear the responsibility to stand resolute in the cultural stream of individualism. Standing firm is difficult if we treat the church like a business because the corporate-church model can't fight the current. We must eliminate language and attitudes that treat the church as a business because they will undermine our efforts to create group-first churches. We must find ways to reorient church members from thinking only about themselves. One way is to encourage believers to serve one another as a natural outcome of the servant ministry of Jesus.

Yes, I know that ministers beg for help regularly, but I want to consider how we ask. How do we motivate people to serve? Is service an obligation? If so, that's okay. I take the trash out each week because I'm obligated to serve our family in that way. Still, my obligation grows out of a sense of commitment to my wife and children rooted in love. I don't take the trash out at Kohl's when I go shopping, since I have no commitment to them.

The church family needs servants in order to thrive. But we also need people to serve as a response to the gospel, not to appease their consciences after a sermon smothered in guilt. Then, as people minister in the joy of Christ, they will find that it's better than being self-focused. Those who serve alongside fellow believers—even others who look, think, and smell differently than they do—often discover that relationships blossom while laboring together in the church. I experienced this in Houston many years ago as a teenage missionary, and the family I gained changed my life.

We also need to tweak our worship lyrics. Worship leaders, do you ever lead a worship set that is entirely me-focused? Do worshipers have a reason to believe that worshiping together is any better than worshiping alone? I challenge you to print out the lyrics to all of the songs you use and search for group language: plural pronouns, references to the church, and exhortations toward unity. You will likely find that individualistic language dominates. If you think that the pool of group-oriented worship songs is too small, you're right. We need creative, Bible-saturated songwriters to pen new worship songs about the family of God and what Christ has done for us. To get the juices flowing, here's a sample from a song I wrote a few years ago: "The spotless groom made pure his bride / Enemies were reconciled / A family formed from orphans lost / When he was on our cross."

Finally, our church members need to know that they are family. But to prove it, we must understand the gospel more fully. And to the gospel we now turn.

4

Adoption, Not Membership

The Theological Basis of the Family of God

Rights of Membership: Every active/resident member shall have the right to participate in the following matters: The annual budget of the church, the disposition of all or substantially all of the assets of the Church, the merger or dissolution of the Church, acquisition of property, and amendments to the Articles of Incorporation or Bylaws of the Church.

—SAMPLE MEMBERSHIP DOCUMENT FROM A BAPTIST STATE CONVENTION OFFICE

GROWING UP, I NEVER had a chance. My brother, Nathan, was (and still is) five years older than me, so I couldn't win a wrestling match, a board game, or an argument during the earliest years of our relationship. We had a few ups, like hiking in the New Mexico mountains together, and lots of downs, like him dragging me down the stairs by my ankles or me knocking him down with a shovel. All of that changed, though, in the summer of 1998.

That summer, my family moved across southern Missouri from Sikeston to Springfield. I would soon begin seventh grade, and my brother was starting his senior year of high school. We left behind friends and family to start a new life in southwest Missouri. The only problem was that my brother and I were both introverts, so making new friends wasn't automatic. My seventh-grade year was one of the loneliest of my life, so who else did I turn to but my brother. We wandered around Springfield or played games at home because all we had was one another. I didn't realize it at the time, but that miserable period would shape my view of family. Only when I desperately needed them did I appreciate that families stick together. Even if the rest of the world let me down, I could count on my family.

I never stopped to ask how I became a Kimbrough. I didn't sign a non-disclosure agreement or agree to contribute 25 percent of my time to family chores. There was no class on how to love my parents. To this day, I don't question if my mom will watch my kids while I write or wonder whether my dad will want to go to a Springfield Cardinals baseball game if I get free tickets. We're family. So, unless there is a reason they can't, I know they'll be there. And the same is true for my kids. My wife and I didn't weigh the pros and cons of sticking with Koen when he was hospitalized as a one-year-old. No, we stayed by his side day and night without being told to. I know that not everyone enjoys the blessing of a faithful family, but I think that, deep down, we all know that families should care for one another through the ups and downs of life.

In this chapter, I want to explore the doctrinal foundation of the family of God. What binds us together? Are we really siblings, or is it all pretend? We will see that the basis of our familial unity is not a contrived set of forms and procedures. Our unity grows out of the very nature of the gospel.

IF THE CHURCH IS A BUSINESS, WE'RE HEADED TOWARD BANKRUPTCY

Scientists recently raised a warning flag over a new epidemic plaguing the West. Researchers say this epidemic is more harmful than obesity or inactivity and is equally as dangerous as smoking fifteen cigarettes a day.[1] Don't worry: this one didn't start with a monkey in an African jungle. Instead, it began the day Adam and Eve disobeyed God's singular command in the garden of Eden and, as a consequence of their sin, realized they were naked and ashamed. The epidemic that began that dark day was loneliness.

A "loneliness epidemic" may sound overdramatic, but scientists warn that the threat of loneliness is real. A recent article on forbes.com reported, "According to two leading researchers, loneliness triggers an inflammatory response and threatens our immune system. These changes can even be

1. "Loneliness Research."

detected at the cellular level. As one of the researchers said, 'The level of toxicity from loneliness is stunning.'"[2] That's right. Loneliness is poisonous! It has the same effect on the human immune system as a virus or infection. Other studies agree that lonely people are more likely to develop chronic disease and have a harder time fighting off everyday illnesses.[3] To recap, a sense of isolation from other people can change our bodies at the cellular level in the same way sickness does. Loneliness isn't just a sad feeling to get over. It is a mental, physical, and spiritual problem with only one real solution: the gospel-rooted family of God.

Why Join a Church?

I believe the most profound question of our age is, Why should I join a church? Older generations didn't ask this question because they were content with a sense of obligation. Everyone should go to church, so why question it? But things have changed. The coronavirus caused many long-time churchgoers to ask for the first time if they needed the church. Many believers admit that attending a worship service is good and right. But is the church essential?

I fear that few churchgoers (and few pastors) could explain why the church is indispensable other than arguing that Hebrews 10:25 commands believers not to give up meeting together. You should go to church because you just should. God said so in the Bible (the divine version of every parent's favorite answer, "Because I said so!"). The dreadful result is that the body of Christ becomes dismembered as individual body parts (or *members*) fail to unite as a complete representation of Jesus, one body. Personal sanctification suffers, and corporate prayer disappears because believers see no need to gather. Pieces of spiritual iron move to and fro but fail to rub close enough to sharpen one another (see Prov 27:17).

Worst of all, if Jesus was correct (he was, by the way), the lost world has no idea that each of us individually follows him. Jesus told the Twelve, "By this everyone will know that you are my disciples, if you love one another" (John 13:35 CSB). How would unbelievers recognize that some people worship Jesus? Surprisingly, not because believers shout, "I follow Christ." Not through moral purity. Not by helping the poor. Not by posting inspiring verses on Facebook. Not by boycotting companies with immoral policies. Certainly not by wearing Christian swag or blasting Hillsong with windows down at a stoplight. Jesus believed that the neon, flashing billboard

2. Behesti, "Detrimental Effect of Loneliness."
3. Resnick, "Loneliness Actually Hurts."

of genuine faith is and will always be love for fellow believers. How can we grow in our love for one another if we don't gather?

Confusion about the value of the church abounds, especially among younger generations. The unstoppable flow of church data reveals that commitment to a body of believers is disappearing. A 2019 Gallup poll depicts a downward trend over the past two decades: "At the turn of the century, 73 [percent] of U.S. adults with a religious preference belonged to a church, compared with 64 [percent] today." My age group isn't helping the problem. "Millennials who are religious are significantly less likely to belong to a church. Fifty-seven percent of religious millennials belong to a church, compared with 65 [percent] or more in older generations."[4]

The numbers are disappointing, but they don't give us the *why* (which is why I don't always trust stats). For example, some articles cite these statistics and offer various, sometimes conflicting, solutions. But, the poll goes on to summarize personal comments from the respondents that reveal their reasoning. "In addition to the ongoing trends toward declining religiosity, Americans who are religious may also be changing their relationship to churches. *They may not see a need to*, or have a desire to, belong to a church and participate in a community of people with similar religious beliefs."[5] I think the problem with the entire survey is summed up in the phrase "community of people with similar religious beliefs." Honestly, I have no need or desire to hang out with people who merely think as I do. If that's all church is, I'll go it alone.

Back to our question, then. Why should I join a church? The corporate-church model must answer this question, and the family model must, too. You may have noticed that, in this chapter, I have mostly avoided the word *member* to describe those who belong to a particular local church. The reason is that while member is a biblical word (see 1 Cor 12), especially in the context of Paul's body metaphor, I fear that it has taken on a more institutional, business-oriented sense. It's true, you could be a family member, but you might also be a Sam's Club member, an Amazon Prime member, a country club member, an American Airlines Advantage card member, and so on. So, what do we mean when we talk about church members? Do we have a familial root metaphor in the back of our minds? If so, I'm all for keeping the word member. Or, does a group of church members make up an organization, institution, or corporation? If that's the context of membership, we have two problems. The corporate-church model forges no

4. Jones, "U.S. Church Membership Down."
5. Jones, "U.S. Church Membership Down."

inherent links between individual church members and, as a result, prompts no devotion to the church as a whole.

Getting In and Staying In

The process of joining a church reveals a lot about the church's values. So-called "qualifications for church membership" designate the ties that hold church members together and expose what the church must know about you before they let you in. One church I surveyed had five qualifications:

- the individual must be at least eighteen years old,
- must agree with the church's statement of faith,
- must have "personal evidence of salvation,"
- must complete membership classes, and
- must agree to the church's bylaws.

So, what church members share in common, what unites them as a local church, is age, doctrinal positions, class attendance, a pledge to live by the church's rules, and faith in Jesus (assuming that is what number 3 means). The gospel is one-fifth of what makes someone a church member.

If a church presents a list of stated expectations for members, this document also exposes the church's priorities. Five is apparently a magic number in church life because several churches I surveyed endorsed five "membership responsibilities." One church expected the following: attend (so the pastors can meet you), give, pray (alone at home for the church), attend communion services, and attend business meetings. Except for prayer, these expectations could describe the elementary school's PTA or a society of Civil War buffs. Attend events, come to meetings, and give. In all fairness, this church states that communion services are essential because "[communion] binds us together as a believing community," which is true (see 1 Cor 11). But, there is no expectation that church members communicate with one another or share life together in any meaningful way. A church member could meet all requirements but know (and be known by) no one except the pastors.

To be transparent, I'm not immune from treating church involvement like joining a home owners association. Years ago, I created a list of obligations that members would sign to join Springhill. Here is an excerpt from our membership form:

All members commit to unite HEARTS with Springhill:

H—humbly submit to guidance and correction from leadership (Heb 13:17)

E—eagerly give to support the mission of the church (2 Cor 9:6–7)

A—actively attend to engage in fellowship and accountability (Heb 10:24–25)

R—readily go as Christ's verbal witness, undergirded by godly living (Matt 28:18–20)

T—truly grow to maturity while seeking to help others grow (1 Pet 2:2–3)

S—selflessly serve Springhill with joy (Gal 5:13)

Ironically, I now feel the acronym lacks heart. Yes, the A, T, and S are community-oriented, but the whole idea of signing a document promising to have fellowship and serve with joy is nonsense. If I had simply written, "Here are some signs of healthy participation in the church," then fine. The points are biblical and, as I will argue in the final chapter, allow us to hold one another accountable. The acronym might even provide the foundation for an excellent sermon series. But this was the fourth page of a contract that potential members would sign and date, a church leader would approve, and an administrator would file to keep on record—what a strange way to run a family.

Let me briefly mention the church covenant approach. I appreciate the biblical, even familial, language, since it shifts away from the business framework. At the same time, the formalized transactional smell of a church covenant still wreaks of the corporate-church model. In what world do children sign a contract agreeing they will complete pages of listed chores and absolving their parents of all responsibility in the event the child breaks her ankle? Even a bride and groom who publicly recite vows to one another don't usually end the ceremony by signing a detailed contract of enforceable obligations. If TV sitcoms are any indication, *prenup* is a curse word in our society, and the fiancé who mentions it is liable to end up alone. We need to ask why we approach church participation differently. What problem does the contract attempt to solve, and is there a more reasonable solution (assuming Scripture defines it as a problem)?

The sample rights of membership provided by a Baptist state convention draws the curtain on the corporate-church model even better than the contracts mentioned above. The example reads, "Every active/resident member shall have the right to participate in the following matters: The annual budget of the church, the disposition of all or substantially all of the assets of the Church, the merger or dissolution of the Church, acquisition of property, and amendments to the Articles of Incorporation or Bylaws of the Church." Oh boy, sign me up! Why join a church? Well, you get to become a church shareholder and participate in all financial or legal transactions. In this case, we could enjoy better benefits as members of the local Chamber of Commerce than as church members.

I am not so naïve as to ignore the legal and practical concerns a church must address. Families, too, have to deal with budgets, assets, mergers (usually called marriage), and buying and selling property. But they tackle these issues from a different perspective than a governing board. The language of this sample rights of membership does not engender affection for a community of believers. It would motivate no one to sacrifice his desires for the good of the family. Even more, it fails to answer the question, Why join a church? No lonely soul will turn to a Christian community for help if the only benefit to joining a church is the right to participate in budgeting. There has to be more.

IF THE CHURCH IS A FAMILY, THE GOSPEL CREATES SIBLINGS

The corporate-church model treats church membership as a legal transaction. But, a contract cannot engender the affection needed among a body of committed believers. Neither do membership qualifications, expectations, and legal rights help a believer understand why he should join a church. If Paul's epistle to the Galatians is any evidence, a better approach is to focus on the believer's identity in Christ. Paul uses various arguments to bridge the divide between classes of believers, but a central motive for unity is that the church is a family.[6]

From Strangers to Siblings

In Gal 3:23—4:7, Paul recognizes that people who did not grow up the same way struggle to worship side by side. Jewish believers grew up under the law, but their upbringing doesn't mean they are the only ones in a relationship with God. The Greek text of verse 26 starts with a word moved to the front for emphasis: *all*. Paul writes, "*All* of you, in fact, are children of God by faith in Christ Jesus" (Gal 3:26, author's translation). Elsewhere, Paul shows that faith in Christ results in forgiveness of sins, reconciliation with God, justification, and much more. But, here, Paul highlights a central result of gospel proclamation: the creation of a family of God's children.

Our silencing of the family-creating impact of the gospel is problematic. When I see the gospel as a mere transaction between God and me, it

6. On the centrality of 3:26–29, see Moo, *Galatians*, 248.

fails to impact my view of the church. Admittedly, the New Testament uses transactional language at times. The term *redemption* comes from the world of the slave market, for instance. So we joyfully affirm that perspective of salvation. But, Paul also sees faith in Jesus as a family-creating act. Joseph Hellerman writes, "Paul and the other New Testament writers made it quite clear that getting saved and becoming a member of the people of God are inseparable, simultaneous events."[7] Just as marriage creates a new family, so the gospel turns strangers into siblings.

Paul goes on in verse 27 to show that the believer's union with Christ gives birth to the familial unity of the church. As a brilliant communicator, Paul rarely uses phrases like *union with Christ* or *incorporation*, opting instead for vivid metaphors such as putting on a coat (clothed with Christ) or becoming immersed in water (baptized into Christ). Imagine diving from a high cliff into a deep river. When your descent finally stops, you realize that everything around you is water. No part of you is unaffected by the water because the river has become your world for the moment. If the water is cold, you're cold. If the water is moving south, you're now moving south. Since the water is wet, you're wet. The nature of the river becomes your nature when you are fully immersed.

In the same way, when you become a believer, you dive into the river that is Christ Jesus. You're still you, but your world has changed drastically. Now, if Christ died and was raised, then you have died and been raised because you're in him. If Jesus is God's child, then you are now God's child in Christ. His experiences, relationships, and benefits become yours in union with him. Consequently, Paul presents union with Christ as the theological basis for the believer's relationship to God as Father and other believers as siblings. Christ is the Son, so we who are in him are also God's children. And if we share the same Father, then we're siblings.

The beauty of the Christian family is that Jesus is our only family trait. We don't need to be the same age, skin color, or gender. Not every member needs to crave sushi or support the Kansas City Chiefs because we have Christ. Paul's claim in verse 28 is revolutionary: "There is neither Jew nor Greek, there is neither slave nor free man, there is neither male nor female; for you are all one in Christ Jesus" (NASB). Paul speaks to three significant barriers in the ancient world that kept different groups from interacting in public. Ethnic, social, and gender-based divisions were meant to protect superior parties from society's inferiors. But the gospel turns rejects into royalty. And it turned the neat categorical boxes of ancient society upside down. The revolutionary part of Paul's message is that Paul redraws family

7. Hellerman, *When Church Was Family*, 123.

lines around Christ alone and, consequently, makes all family members equal heirs of the inheritance. Only in Christ could a Jewish male slave and a freeborn Greek woman become family. Only the gospel can turn divided people into spiritual siblings.

Joining the family of God comes with benefits, to which Paul turns in the following verses. Verse 29 serves as a transition to the next section of Galatians. Paul writes, "Now if you are part of Christ, then you are the 'seed' of Abraham, heirs according to promise" (Gal 3:29, author's translation). How does union with Christ change the believer's heritage? He doesn't simply give us blessings and benefits for believing in him. No, those who believe share in his heritage and inheritance. If these truths don't excite you, it may be because, like me, you don't expect a vast earthly inheritance. My parents have worked hard all their lives in ministry, teaching, and other jobs, but their efforts haven't produced dramatic wealth. We aren't like America's wealthiest family, the Waltons.

The family who runs Walmart is worth over $160 billion (that's 160,000,000,000).[8] Adoption into their family would mean becoming an heir to mansions, ranches, Park Avenue condos, museums, expensive cars, and artwork by Andy Warhol and Georgia O'Keefe. Even more valuable is the family business, which brings in approximately $12,000 every minute of the year. But the Waltons didn't create the world. The Waltons don't cause every human heart to beat. The Waltons don't provide the sun and rain needed to grow all of the world's food. They aren't the authority over all of life and existence. They don't own all things. They don't have the power to restore all that is broken in this world or to forgive sins or to promise eternal life after death. But our Father does! And in Christ, we are heirs of a glorious inheritance.

From Slaves to Sons

The opportunity to take on a new identity in Christ is part of a distinct era of history. In Gal 4:1–3, Paul pictures the time before Christ using the analogy of a young son (humanity) waiting to come of age as a true heir of his father (the era of salvation by faith in Christ). In the ancient world, wealthy families bought slaves to keep young children in line. These enslaved tutors guaranteed the children would get to school safely, behave during instruction, and complete all assignments (compare the tutor in Gal 3:23–25). The slave would beat failure out of the child with a stick, giving tutors a poor reputation in ancient literature. It seems that ancient poets

8. Hanbury, "Meet the Waltons."

and philosophers still had a bone to pick with their tutors long after aging out from under their authority. According to Paul, a child under the tutor's scrutiny felt more like a slave than a future owner of all his father's wealth (4:1). Likewise, Paul's audience felt more like slaves than God's children at one time, but then Christ, the Son, came (4:2–3). At the perfect time, the Father dissolved the slave-like relationship and provided all of the benefits of sonship through Jesus.

In Gal 4:4–5, Paul writes in a rhetorically creative way that links together two ideas: "God sent forth His Son . . . that we might receive the adoption as sons" (NASB). Jesus's sonship becomes our sonship because the gospel results in adoption. In the ancient world, adoption was common even for sons who had living parents. Poor people had few opportunities to move up in the world and provide their children with a better future. No college degrees or small business loans existed to bridge the canyon-sized gap between rich and poor. One of the few weapons in the arsenal of poor parents was convincing a well-to-do father to adopt an impoverished child (almost exclusively a son). The high-status father would gain a hardworking family member and heir to continue the family line. The former parents might receive payment for the adopted child. And the new son would enjoy all of the legal and relational privileges of a biological son. Ancient adoption, then, benefited all parties.

When it comes to the gospel, on the other hand, adoption is one-sided. God needs nothing and no one, but he generously offers the full relational and practical privileges of sonship through Christ. Paul identifies the relational benefits of adoption in verse 6, writing, "Because you are sons, God has sent forth the Spirit of His Son into our hearts, crying, 'Abba! Father!'" (NASB). God directs the Spirit of his Son, Jesus, to dwell within us, so that we might relate to the Father in a unique, intimate way. The adopted child addresses God the Father not only as Master or Lord but also as *Daddy*. Scot McKnight describes the multiple facets of the term *abba* this way, "Calling God *Abba* is the most intimate language of the family in the Jewish world. This was the first term a Jewish child learned (along with *imma*, 'mommy'), and it can be translated 'daddy.'"[9] Paul (like Jesus) refers to God as *Abba* to show God's loving, approachable, fatherly nature and the beautiful simplicity of a relationship with him. Like Jesus, we enjoy an affectionate relationship with God.

But the term *abba* is not void of familial obligation. McKnight adds, "While 'daddy' is accurate, there is more to it than the language of a child. The father, the *abba*, in Judaism was also a commanding authority figure

---

9. McKnight, *Galatians*, 46.

for the Jewish family, and children were taught never to disagree with and always to honor him."[10] I understand the sentiment. Growing up, my family lived in homes with basements. Dungeon-like settings seem to breed violence in boys, so the fights between my brother and me usually exploded in the basement. Inevitably, we would cross whatever invisible line demanded that my dad put an end to our bickering, and we would hear the most terrifying sound we could imagine: my dad stomping across the floor above us. At the thunder of his heavy footfalls, we immediately reformed our ways out of a healthy fear of his disapproval (even though, in retrospect, he was overly kind). In the same way, we must remember that we cry *Abba* because the Spirit of Jesus cries out from within us, a Spirit who exemplifies obedience to the Father. We can expect the Spirit to push us toward obedience because submission to our *Abba* is the expected result of spiritual adoption.

Salvation through Faith as an Inheritance

In addition to the relational benefits of adoption, Paul recalls the practical privileges that children of God enjoy. Paul writes in verse 7, "Therefore you are no longer a slave, but a son; and if a son, then an heir through God." Paul's language is a bit confusing here, so let me lay it out for you. Slavery depicts the era before Christ, before the day darkness covered the earth, the ground shook, and Jesus breathed his last. Now that Jesus has died and risen, slaves become sons and enjoy inheritance rights, chiefly access to God via faith. We could compare this to a Jewish boy's *bar mitzvah*. The boy turns thirteen and is now responsible for God's commandments and is allowed to participate in worship. For Paul, the whole world had a *bar mitzvah* when Christ came. Childhood under the law ended, and adulthood under faith began. Even more amazing is that faith in Jesus allows the believer to claim parts of the inheritance now (sort of like the prodigal son, except our Father freely offers an early down payment).

The present inheritance includes salvation by faith for any person, Jew or not. Paul sometimes speaks of different sorts of inheritance—the promise of enjoying God's presence forever or the Spirit's ministry in the believer's life—but here, the present inheritance is the new way believers can relate to God by faith. Imagine a father passing down an ID badge to his children that guarantees immediate access to the president. Through Christ, God has given us access to himself, and the only ID we need is faith. Paul highlights faith (which comes from the same Greek root as *belief*) just a chapter earlier, writing, ". . . just like Abraham who *believed* God, and it was credited to

10. McKnight, *Galatians*, 46–47.

him for righteousness? You know, then, that those who have *faith*, these are Abraham's sons. Now the Scripture saw in advance that God would justify the Gentiles by *faith* and proclaimed the gospel ahead of time to Abraham, saying, All the nations will be blessed through you. Consequently, those who have *faith* are blessed with Abraham,who had *faith*" (Gal 3:6–9 CSB, emphasis added).

Long before Paul's day, God promised that he would bless all nations through Abraham. To everyone's surprise, though, the blessing did not come through the law God gave to Israel but rather by faith. Paul rejoiced that "Faith Day" had arrived. He joyfully proclaimed that adopted children of God enjoy their inheritance—the opportunity to draw near to God by faith in Jesus—right now.

Paul's brief comments about spiritual adoption are profound. For Paul, adoption depicts not only what God saved us from but what he saved us into. We can easily find examples of what we are saved from. For example, Romans 3 highlights that the righteous Judge has forgiven our sin. But just because a judge lets someone go free does not mean he has invited the defendant to join his own family. In other words, forgiveness and freedom—glorious and biblical as they are—aren't the same as entering a positive relationship with God. A biblical view of adoption, then, is a crucial aspect of salvation imagery. The believer is not a mere freed slave wandering through life thankful but alone. Rather, the freed slave has become a beloved son in a family full of siblings.

SWAPPING METAPHORS: PUTTING "FAMILY" AND "MEMBER" BACK TOGETHER

American Evangelicals consistently use the term *member* to describe someone committed to a local church, and I don't recommend we ditch the term. However, we must intentionally correct misguided, corporate-church views of what membership means. And it all starts with a more robust understanding of the gospel and its blessing of familification.

Familification

Why join a church? The corporate-church model offers church members legal rights and responsibilities but fails to answer the question. But the family model is rooted in a critical outcome of the gospel, what Joseph Hellerman calls familification. Hellerman recommends that we talk about familification (the formation of a family in Christ) at least as often as we speak of justification or redemption.[11] The problem is theological: we have downplayed union with Christ compared to other biblical images like redemption. I imagine our individualistic sensibilities like the language of pardon and freedom from sin more than they like the idea of losing ourselves in the identity of Jesus. Yet, the language of union with Christ springs from the New Testament soil constantly, so we cannot ignore it and its fruit of familification. To ignore familification through union with Christ is to follow in Peter's flawed footsteps in Galatians 2 and, as a result, to belittle the gospel.

According to Paul, the gospel creates a family, a church of brothers and sisters who worship their *Abba* together. In Christ, diverse strangers become siblings. And since believers are siblings, church gatherings give the family quality time together. If the church were a business, I would want to participate as much as I want to hang out at a shoe store. I would communicate with fellow members as much as I talk with other customers at the mall food court. But if the church is a family, then services and events provide the opportunity to enjoy my brothers and sisters, to reunite after time apart. I love my physical family and want to spend time with them. If the church is a family, I join because I love the people and want to be with them.

If you have not experienced a healthy home life, the concept of the church family may not appeal to you. But the gospel has the power to change your heart, to restore hope that healthy relationships are possible. Hellerman writes, "Apart from Christ, I have no solid basis on which to build healthy relationships with my fellow human beings. But as a child in God's family, I belong to a group where relational integrity and wholeness are to be the norm."[12] The gospel reconciles us both to God and man, forming the church as the most effective antidote against the poisonous effects of loneliness, conflict, and mistrust.

The Church Family Member

As we reclaim the doctrine of familification, we must also redefine church membership. Again, I don't suggest we abandon membership language, but it would help to add words like *family* or *body* for clarification. Ask around and see what your church thinks of membership. Play a word association game with those in your congregation. "I say 'member,' you say . . . ?" If they say *organization* or *club*, you may have a problem. If they say *family*, then

11. Hellerman, *When Church Was Family*, 132.

12. Hellerman, *When Church Was Family*, 127.

breathe a sigh of relief. Remember that the language we use matters because it often reveals our root metaphors. If we desire to promote the root metaphor "The church is a family," we must use our language consistently and purposefully. This applies to the way pastors present new family members to the church and how leaders describe what church membership means.

One way to reshape our language around the family model is to remove all talk of qualifications and membership rights. Families today don't use these words to define their relationships, so the church shouldn't either. Doing so can only lead to confusion about the nature of membership. Along the same lines, we need to think about what is required to become a church family member. We must let gospel-rooted theology dictate church practices.

So, what makes someone a member of God's family? Must you sign a form? No, because faith in Christ is an act of the heart. Do you have to be the minimum legal age of a voting American? I don't think so, since Jesus scolded his disciples for keeping children from him. What about agreeing to all of the local church's doctrinal assumptions and bylaws? Theology is essential, and a church must stand as a pillar of truth. But if the only family trait that unites us is faith in Jesus, then whether someone takes a premillennial or amillennial view of Revelation should not determine whether a church welcomes him into the family. My point is that the gospel should not comprise a mere 20 percent of our membership qualifications because the gospel is not 20 percent of what makes someone a Christian. The gospel is everything.

Getting Connected

To be practical, I'm suggesting that we reshape our membership processes to look more like determining whom you should marry. Emily and I started spending time together when I was sixteen and she was fourteen (she couldn't date until she turned fourteen). I had dated a few girls before her, but Emily was different. She was special. As we spent time together, my concern was not how she could serve me or which chores I would do if we got married. The relationships came first. We got along well, enjoyed spending time together, and grew to love each other deeply. Eventually, I gave her a one-question survey to determine if we would become husband and wife. I asked, "Will you marry me?" By God's grace, she said yes. At our wedding a few months later, we committed to love each other no matter what, and we strive every day to keep that commitment. The process for most married people sounds something like this. Even with variations of timing, personality, and circumstances, Western couples typically get to know one another, discover a unique connection, and then choose to commit to one another with that same simple question, "Will you marry me?" Why can't we do the same with a church?

I understand that not every local church is ideal for every believer. But, a believer could date a few churches, if need be, to find one he can grow to love. By the way, dating a church requires more time and personal investment than church shopping, just as finding a girlfriend is more complicated than picking out an apple. Once a believer has found a church family that is a good match, he should get to know her well. He does so not only by showing up to Sunday services but also by serving, attending events, asking people out to lunch on Sundays, joining a small group, and so on. Once he's sure this is the family to which he wants to commit, the church should ask one simple question. Have you been saved by grace through faith in Jesus Christ? If so, he's qualified and should commit his life to the local church family for better or worse. No prenups required.

We need to eliminate the trend of signing an exhaustive legal membership contract as a prerequisite to participating fully in church life. One purpose of a contract is to provoke a sense of obligation to the local church, which is a noble goal, even if not a worthy means to attain it. The family model is also heavy on duty, but duty rooted in our identity as siblings. As a parent, I have to provide for my children, correct them, and care for them with the love of Jesus. The duties of parenting aren't always fun. Yet, parenting can provide a deep-seated joy, unlike most other obligations. The same is true for responsibilities that arise out of the familial model. Those who preach and teach should challenge new family members to love and care for the family as a joyful obligation. We also must remind established members of what it means to love their siblings well.

Our efforts to change root metaphors won't make selfish people into perfect Christians, nor will it automatically turn our broken congregations into glimmering gospel lights. Church family members will need reminders of what love in action looks like, just as husbands, wives, parents, and children often do. All relationships are messy because sin still infects our lives. But signing a contract doesn't help. If it did, our churches would have arrived already. So, maybe we should try a different approach that conforms more closely to the biblical root metaphor: the church is a family.

Let me return to two diagnostic questions church leaders should consider. What problem does a contract attempt to solve? And is there a more reasonable solution to the problem? Maybe leaders use a contract to teach people about the church's values or doctrines. If so, a better solution would be to share a meal with potential new members and take time to teach them about the church. Think of it as a date.

Does the contract provide information to improve communication? Good communication is a worthy goal that married couples have attained since the beginning of time without forcing each other to sign impersonal documents. Does the contract provide a way to control members so they conform to the leaders' expectations? If so, we must look to Scripture to see if this is a biblical goal, and we'll find it is not. A helpful list of pastoral obligations appears in 1 Peter 5, including the call to shepherd a congregation eagerly, "nor yet as *lording it over* those allotted to your charge, but proving to be examples to the flock" (1 Pet 5:3 NASB, emphasis added). Pastors and siblings in Christ should exhort, encourage, and rebuke one another, no contract needed. In all, I can think of no benefit of a membership form that a personal, familial conversation cannot attain. I know I sound old-fashioned, but we should have face-to-face conversations with prospective members about church life, theology, and anything else that actually matters. Find out their passions and gifts. There's nothing on a form that we can't discover through a conversation. The only actual cost is time.

The Value of an Ideal

Despite our common adoption, siblings in Christ will sometimes hurt one another, just like my biological brother and I did. We will refuse to share our toys and argue about who did the most chores. Yet, the reality of conflict does not invalidate the biblical truth that the church is a family (just as the existence of evil does not disprove God's goodness). If anything, the pain caused by a broken relationship reveals that God created us for community. Otherwise, soured relationships would not affect us.

Because we all know churches mired in disunity, we must hold the familial model even higher as our gospel-rooted ideal for church life. People need a reason to stick together. The apostle Paul believed the gospel could turn believers from two races who hated and distrusted one another into a family. He wrote Galatians to bring Jewish and gentile Christians together, trusting the Spirit's working in their midst to solve problems that rules failed to correct (Gal 5:13–26). Some listeners likely critiqued Paul's letter as idealistic, thinking the apostle couldn't see past the utopian cloud of his theology to the painful reality of life on the ground. Yet, the stark ending of Galatians tells a different story. Paul writes, "From now on let no one cause trouble for me, for I bear on my body the brand-marks of Jesus" (Gal 6:17 NASB). Like Jesus, Paul knew suffering, but it didn't prevent him from holding the Galatians to a high standard: "For you were called to freedom, *brethren*; only do not turn your freedom into an opportunity for the flesh, but through love serve one another" (Gal 5:13 NASB, emphasis added). Faith in the outworking of the gospel leads Paul to issue these seemingly impossible commands.

Like Paul, we must defend a biblical picture of church membership that explains why believers should join a church. Membership in the family of God is one of many praiseworthy results of the gospel, and we should celebrate it. Thank God he did not leave us alone but gave us adopted brothers and sisters. But questions remain. What is the family supposed to do? What drives the church family from week to week? We will turn to these questions in the next chapter.

5

Growing Healthier, Not Merely Bigger

The Purpose of the Family of God

The numerical approach is essential to understanding church growth. The Church is made up of countable people and there is nothing particularly spiritual in not counting them. Men use the numerical approach in all worthwhile human endeavor. Industry, commerce, finance, research, government, invention and a thousand other lines of enterprise derive great profit and much of their stability in development from continual measurement. Without it they would feel helpless and blindfolded.

—Don McGavran

The most difficult season of my life so far began late in the summer of 2013. In early August, my father-in-law's oncologist uttered words we knew were coming but for which we could never prepare: "It's time for hospice." That simple sentence means hope is lost, that God has not answered prayers for healing. What do you do when you know the days are short? How do you go on with everyday life—laundry or mowing the lawn—when someone's life is ending? How do you celebrate a man's birthday when you know he won't use the gifts you give him for long? Anyone who has traversed this valley knows the questions seem to multiply with each passing day, while no answers reveal themselves.

The following week, our senior pastor resigned. Seriously. I didn't blame him for taking a new position, but the timing stank. He had hired me years before, believing that a know-it-all twenty-one-year-old college student could handle the load. We had (barely) weathered major ministry storms together through the years, leaving both of us with lifelong scars. I know he hated to resign at that moment, but I was too shocked to care how he felt. While I was trying to lead my family through the valley of the shadow of death, I now had to carry a church of three hundred souls on my back as the lone pastor of Springhill. The trek was too much for a young pastor like me.

In case you're wondering, the story doesn't end there. Two weeks later, I began my first PhD seminars at Midwestern Baptist Theological Seminary, entering an intense period of academic training as my family and church were falling apart. Every Monday morning, I woke up at 5:00 a.m., made the three-hour trip to Kansas City, sleepwalked through doctoral seminars until 5:30 p.m., and got home at 8:30 p.m. I had been a 4.0 GPA student throughout college and most of seminary, but all I could do was survive that semester. The professor in my advanced Greek class often wrote "grace" on my homework rather than give me an actual grade. That wasn't how I planned to begin my doctoral studies.

On Sunday, September 1, my mentor preached his final sermon as the senior pastor of Springhill. My father-in-law, Dean, took his last breath four days later on September 5. Two days after that, on September 7, I led worship for one of the most inspiring funeral services I have ever witnessed. We did a bluesy rendition of "Amazing Grace" that Dean would have loved. We said goodbye to a spiritual giant that day. The next day, I led worship and preached the first sermon of Springhill's interim period as the church simultaneously mourned the resignation of a pastor and the death of a long-time servant and leader. During the sermon, I sat on a stool in tears and reminded myself (while Springhill listened) that Jesus was the pastor we all needed at that moment, that God had not abandoned us.

I'm not sure I believed my own words that morning. But then came Sunday afternoon. No literary genius could craft a novel with an event as surprising as what happened next. That afternoon, barely twenty-four hours after burying my father-in-law, we found out my wife was pregnant for the first time.

During the last weeks of my father-in-law's life, my wife, Emily, had felt ill. We weren't complete fools, but every pregnancy test came back negative. Surely her nausea was a natural response to the intense grief she felt. She was treading water in a sea of sorrow, which would exhaust anyone. So, Emily had eaten Tums like they were candy and continued putting one foot in front of the other. Not until that Sunday afternoon, after a week of misery, did we realize that something was off. One pregnancy test later, and we were jumping around the room, crying like buffoons, thanking God for the beautiful gift of a baby who was our rainbow after the flood, our mountain of transfiguration where God allowed us to see a glimpse of his glory. The pregnancy gave our mourning family hope that God had not abandoned us, that sorrow may last for the night, but joy comes in the morning. Rylie came nine months later and has grown into a beautiful, compassionate, self-sufficient little girl. And unlike everyone else in her biological family, she is left-handed, just like her Papa Dean was.

I tell that story because it shows God's extraordinary kindness and perfect timing. But it also reveals the kind of growth we should celebrate. We didn't rejoice over our pregnancy because it represented a 50 percent increase in our family size. No one silently sneered at us because our family had three members while theirs had six. Many of our friends have more children than we do, and we don't envy them! When it comes to family, we don't celebrate numerical growth as if seven is better than three. We celebrate life. We celebrate human beings. We celebrate God's perfectly timed gift. And I would not feel more successful as a parent if our family grew from four to forty.

Seven years later, our family is complete (Lord willing), and the word *growth* has taken on a new significance. Some aspects are quantifiable: fine motor skills, vocabulary, height, the number of concerned emails from the kindergarten teacher, and so on. But I find it difficult to measure the kinds of growth I pray for. Do my kids love Jesus? Are they compassionate? Do they understand Scripture better than they did a few months ago? Are we increasing in affection as a family? Do my children love the church? These are the most accurate measures of my family's success, whether I can easily gauge the results or not.

A family's view of success overlaps very little with the goals of Chevrolet, Google, or Ben & Jerry's. I don't mean to imply that corporations have sinful desires. A family simply doesn't define success the same way a business does. But what about the church? What defines a successful church or pastor? How do we know when God has blessed a congregation? Most often, we look to numbers.

IF THE CHURCH IS A BUSINESS, NUMBERS ARE EVERYTHING

Don McGavran fired the shot that maimed the church's sense of identity. In his defense, he aimed for a greater foe—the problem of lostness in America—but the church suffered collateral damage, and our view of what the church *is* has not recovered. Considered by many as the father of the church growth movement, McGavran was not a businessman but a missionary. He watched as the gospel seed took root in the non-Western world, particularly India, freeing people from slavery to sin and filling church buildings beyond capacity. As an astute missionary, McGavran determined to study patterns among the largest churches that other missionaries could replicate. Along the way, McGavran authored several popular books on church growth and founded two West Coast church growth programs that became launching points for a movement.

Missiologists today define McGavran's legacy using three principles.[1] First, McGavran states that unbelievers need to hear the gospel and respond to the Spirit's prompting. None would deny the biblical basis for McGavran's first principle. Conversion is the foundation of spiritual growth, and evangelism is the God-ordained tool for conversion. Where believers fail to proclaim the gospel, growth will not occur. In fact, every mention of numerical growth in Acts follows the proclamation of the gospel or the direct work of the Spirit.[2] So, I gladly concur when the church growth movement lauds evangelism—going out with the gospel—as the means of numerical growth. Yet, evangelism isn't the only banner church growth gurus raise. Otherwise, we wouldn't need shelves of books, endless conferences, and booming church growth institutes.

The Quality of Quantification

McGavran's second principle is that the church must quantify and analyze church growth. McGavran heralds the corporate-church paradigm, writing, "The numerical approach is essential to understanding church growth. The Church is made up of countable people and there is nothing particularly

1. McIntosh, *Evaluating Church Growth Movement*, 15–16.

2. Acts 2:41, 47 following Peter's Pentecost sermon; 4:4 after the arrest of Peter and John for preaching the gospel; 5:14 as signs and wonders affirm the apostles' witness; 5:42—6:1 as the apostles preach in the temple and from house to house; 6:7 in Stephen's speaking ministry accompanied by miraculous signs (see v. 10); 9:31 by the work of the Spirit; 11:21, 24 as men scattered after Stephen's death preached the gospel abroad; and 16:5 in association with Paul's itinerant ministry.

spiritual in not counting them."[3] According to McGavran, the church must chart the circumstances of both growth and decline for two reasons. First, counting people is spiritually neutral. Quantification is like a hammer, a morally neutral tool. What matters is the hand that swings it. Yet, is Mc-Gavran's presupposition accurate? Is there no opportunity for sin to take root in the numerical approach?

I think a focus on quantifying church growth carries inherent risks, the most prominent being pastoral deism. What I mean by pastoral deism is the implicit belief that Jesus created the church and then retired to his heavenly waiting room until his grand return at the end. Like the deists of the Enlightenment era who proposed that God, like a divine clockmaker, set the world into motion and then allowed creation to govern itself, McGavran risks treating church growth as the pastor's sole responsibility rather than God's. God set the church in motion. Pastors grow the church by analyzing data points and plagiarizing what seems to produce success.

Church growth gurus study trends in the largest churches, believing that every megachurch's success is reproducible. However, reproducibility implies producibility. A talented forger can reproduce the Mona Lisa because da Vinci first painted the famous piece. The same forger cannot reproduce a cumulonimbus cloud because humans have never produced them. If we cannot produce something, we can't reproduce it either.

By claiming that we can reproduce First Church's numerical growth using three simple strategies, we imply that First Church produced their increase. Do what they did, and your church numbers will skyrocket. This is pastoral deism: God started the church, but my brilliance and work ethic will keep the doors open. When quantification produces pastoral deism, we may no longer consider it a neutral tool. Even at its best, quantification remains theologically risky because it removes God from the picture.

The second reason church leaders should chart growth and decline is that it works, according to McGavran. Like the movement he spawned, McGavran champions a philosophy of bald pragmatism. The logic is simple.

- Cause: Pastor Tom initiates an advertising campaign for his new series, "Ten Tips for the Tired Teacher," using social media and commercial spots on the local news.

- Effect: during the series, the attendance at Pastor Tom's services doubles.

- Implication: you connect the cause with the effect and determine that you, too, should advertise your next "Practical Advice" series to increase your church's attendance.

3. McGavran, *Understanding Church Growth*, 83.

In his 1970 church growth manifesto, *Understanding Church Growth*, McGavran offered a strategic primer for the pastor wishing to increase his church size. He wrote, "With the record of each congregation before him, the student of church growth can concentrate on cases of great growth and those of decline, and probe for the real reasons for each case."[4] What is the real reason for numerical growth or decline? Something the pastor does or doesn't do determines the numerical success of the church, right? This pragmatism is pastoral deism in disguise.

The long-term impact of pragmatism is devastating. One of the many problems with a pragmatic approach to church growth is that pastors only pursue churches with an obvious potential for numerical success—in other words, the increase of both people and dollars. Put yourself in a church planter's shoes. By McGavran's logic, you should prepare for numerical success by studying large churches and identifying trends. The five largest churches in America at the time of writing are, from largest to smallest, Lakewood Church (Joel Osteen), North Point Community Church (Andy Stanley), Life.Church (Craig Groeschel), Gateway Church (Robert Morris), and Willow Creek (formerly Bill Hybels). These churches average nearly 32,000 members, making them Christian empires in their cities.

What, then, is the recipe for success? Well, one trend seems to be the neighborhood where the church building sits.[5] For example, the average cost of purchasing a home near these churches is $750,000. By comparison, the average US home costs just over $250,000. Admittedly, some of these churches first began in garages or schools, but they grew numerically in the womb of affluence. These campuses also exploded in neighborhoods with unusually high percentages of white residents. Although the cities around these churches are only 52 percent white, the residents of these churches' neighborhoods are 76 percent white. That means that the five largest American churches meet in neighborhoods 24 percent whiter than their cities.

Using McGavran's principles, what should we conclude?

- Cause: churches plant in wealthy, white communities.

- Effect: they grow exponentially.

- Implication: you should avoid lower-income, minority, or rural communities if you want to become a "successful" church planter.

---

4 McGavran, *Understanding Church Growth*, 97.

5. These statistics relate to the first or main campus of each church, where these pastors gained the success that allowed them to expand in many other directions. These numbers reflect pre-COVID trends before the housing bubble began. For statistics, see Minnicks, "Largest Churches in America."

The Atlantic conducted comparable research and came to similar conclusions:

> Church life in general seems to be falling along economic lines: Churches of all sizes proliferate the suburbs and the tonier parts of America's urban cores, while in lower income, economically stagnant neighborhoods, churches tend to be very small, very old, and in general, not as active in their community. . . . Churches, especially new churches with young leadership and young congregants, seem to be a feature of stable and upwardly mobile communities. The disadvantaged communities that are most in need of the services churches exist in part to provide cannot afford to start and sustain those churches—and thus they are not getting them.[6]

If the church is a business, we should celebrate these trends. The process is working as it should. Pragmatism has won. This leads us back to McGavran's principles.

Church Growth in Practice

McGavran's third and final principle is that pastors must apply church growth research. Application requires that vocabulary once sequestered within corporate America become common among Christian leaders, terms like goal-setting, mission statement, measurable outcomes, executive (pastor), and so on. Let's consider the first two.

If we replace the word *goal* with *hope*, I'm content. We should hope for God to work powerfully, pray to that end, and play our parts as God directs us. Most church growth experts agree. The problem arises when the adjective *measurable* sneaks in. As Thom Rainer puts it, "Goals must be *measurable*. A vague goal that cannot be measured over a specified time frame is worthless."[7]

If church growth books and conferences have made anything clear, measurable means *numerical*. If measurability is primary, then only a foolish pastor would set a goal that his church members grow in unity this calendar year. The church sets a "worthless" goal, according to Rainer, when it determines to live generously during the Christmas season—that is, unless leaders establish some arbitrary metrics (give away $10,000) as benchmarks of success. Can we quantify whether our church members prayed in a more

---

6. Dodd, "Low-Income Communities Are Struggling."

7. Rainer, *Book of Church Growth*, 267 (emphasis in original), in conversation with Wagner, *Leading Your Church to Growth*, 186–90.

biblical manner this month or increased in gratitude? How do we discern the numerical value of the fruit of the Spirit? Can we quantify a person's worship? We must evaluate these areas, but quantifiable data doesn't paint a complete picture. We need different means of assessment. Thus, measurable goal-setting isn't the "awesome power" Peter Wagner describes it to be.[8] Instead, quantification can become a distraction at best and an idol at worst.

In the same vein, the mission or vision statement has become an essential driving force behind church life. Or at least vision statement creators think so. Reflecting on the typical training for potential church planters, Jason Sexton observes:

> Within the process of preparation, the organization's director of church planting emphasized that it was not the theology of the church (or a theology of mission for that matter) that needed to be emphasized; instead the entrepreneurial church planter's mission (and corresponding vision) were to be the focus. This was partly about branding, but also about keeping the vibrant goal in view, although it's not much different than business strategies from companies like Starbucks or Apple, often touted by church leaders as successful efforts to accomplish any organizational mission, including the church's.[9]

Sexton's implied critique is that biblical theology no longer drives the church's mission, not since the corporate-church model took over. Now, each pastor or church planter senses the responsibility to receive (in some indistinct, mystical way) a vision from God for the church.

Good mission statements merely summarize biblical teaching, usually in the quintessential triad that goes something like, "Love God. Serve the church. Evangelize the unbeliever." It's one part Great Commandment, one part Ephesians 4, and one part Great Commission. That works for me (as long as we recognize the triad isn't unique to any one church). We should summarize the broad themes of Scripture to keep our churches on track.

Still, I'm not sure these statements are as helpful as we think. One touted purpose of a mission statement is to narrow what the church should and shouldn't do. If the senior adult pastor's event doesn't fit the vision, he shouldn't host it. The problem is that the better mission statements—those that summarize major themes in Scripture—aren't specific enough to eliminate any activity or plan. Church putt-putt golf tournament? We're serving the church with a family-friendly event. Church-sponsored Metallica cover

---

8. Wagner, *Leading Your Church to Growth*, 186; as cited in Rainer, *Book of Church Growth*, 266–67.

9. Sexton, "Introduction," 8.

band? We're reaching out to unbelievers. If everything fits the vision, doesn't the statement lose its value?

Some churches go to the opposite extreme, generating an exclusive, narrow vision statement that leaves half of their community out on the streets. Often, these are pastors who don't want to interact with their oldest congregants, so the vision becomes "Reaching young families for Christ." What happens when the senior saints get lost in the shuffle? "Old people shouldn't complain," these ministers reason, "since the church has formally left them behind." The vision statement says so.

More optimistically, a pastor sometimes holds deep affection for a certain demographic: struggling married couples, single parents, successful entrepreneurs, and so on. I applaud a pastor who can minister to those that others might ignore. Outreach ministries and discipleship classes targeting such groups can transform individuals and their communities. Still, I question whether pastors should narrow their church's vision statement to a particular demographic. After all, the early church could have split into Jewish and gentile churches, but the apostles found ways to compromise so all could participate (see Acts 15:1–35).

Where does the single person connect in a "young family" church? How do the elderly fit in a church whose mission is to reach young parents? What of the poor person in the church designed for wealthy business people? And while I know the Great Commission (Matt 28:19–20) is not the only biblical mission statement, I wonder whether we have the right to narrow our individual churches' visions any smaller than "Go and make disciples of all nations." Maybe our solution to the lack of clarity in our churches is not a specific vision statement focused on a limited demographic but a recommitment to the mission of God seen in Scripture.[10]

IF THE CHURCH IS FAMILY, GROWTH ISN'T JUST NUMBERS

I recently heard an executive pastor say that he led one-to-one's every month with his entire staff. If you aren't familiar with one-to-one's, God has blessed you. They are controlled conflicts where you and your boss discuss what you did well, what you did poorly, and how to improve. I would say one-to-ones are bad, but that wouldn't be fair. They're terrible! I'm kidding: *bad* is fine.

Evaluation and correction are biblical and, when done with love, can powerfully aid personal growth. However, business ideology often

10. We don't have space to evaluate various views on the church's mission. For a primer, see Sexton, "Introduction."

determines what performance data the executive pastor addresses in one-to-ones. The youth pastor must prove on paper that he is growing (in other words, *increasing*) his ministry's influence. The worship leader must show that she has cut costs. Every pastor should demonstrate measurable improvements in his department: more volunteers, fewer dropouts, and more ministry engagement. Are such demands biblical?

Not Unbiblical, but Non-Biblical

As I thought about this well-meaning executive pastor's approach to ministry, I considered that Jesus decreased the footprint of his ministry when the crowds grew too large. I searched the New Testament epistles for a results-oriented, quantifiable measure of church success and found nothing. I combed Acts and considered the numbers Luke records, but I found only the Spirit changing hearts through gospel preaching, not a goal-setting church meeting their marks. That's when I realized that church growth principles did not motivate early Christians. Take Thom Rainer's honest assessment of Peter Wagner's church growth strategies:

> Rather than accept Wagner's premise that there is a "biblical pattern of consecrated pragmatism [and] . . . strategy planning," it is probably best to consider strategy planning as more pragmatic than biblical, while affirming its value in church growth endeavors. When Wagner speaks of the advantages of having a strategy for church growth, his points are much like those one would hear in business. His points are not unbiblical, and they are concerned with the goal of winning the most people to Christ. Their sources, however, are more from pragmatic concern than solid biblical evidence.[11]

I sincerely appreciate Rainer's honesty. Too many church growth experts try to validate their strategies with ill-fitting biblical prooftexts. Proverbs 29:18a takes pride of place: "Where there is no vision, the people perish" (KJV). We might assume God inspired this text so that nearly three thousand years later, a pastor would retreat to the mountains and wait for a vision statement to come down from God on the wings of a fiery dove. Sadly, we would be wrong (though the mountains sound nice). In Prov 29:18a, the word *vision* refers to the act of revealing God's word to the congregation of Israel, much like the word *preaching* today. And *perish* means something like

---

11. Wagner, *Strategies for Church Growth*, 30–32, as cited in Rainer, *Big Book of Church Growth*, 269.

run wild. So, Proverbs 29:18a does not apply to modern vision statements but to pastors whose sermons prevent sin from spreading throughout the church.[12]

Church growth strategies are not rooted in Scripture, but the New Testament epistles often record commands and prayers for growth. Just not measurable growth. Notice the areas the apostles hope their churches will "grow in" (also using the near synonym "abound in"): hope (Rom 15:13), grace and righteousness (2 Cor 9:8–10), faith (2 Cor 10:15), love (Phil 1:9; 1 Thess 3:12; 2 Thess 1:3), knowledge (Col 1:10; 2 Pet 3:18), prayer (Heb 13:19), maturity (1 Pet 2:2), and character (2 Pet 1:8). These earliest church leaders didn't create goals for attendance, budgets, or staff members. They didn't even demand that their churches set projections for yearly baptisms or evangelistic touches. Instead, they emphasized the traits of spiritual growth that are tough to quantify but foolish to ignore. The result was that the church grew spiritually and numerically! So, we can affirm Rainer's claim that church growth principles aren't unbiblical in the sense that the Bible does not prohibit goal setting, for example. Yet, the underlying values of the church growth movement—values like measurability, reproducibility, and pragmatism—contradict a biblical view of real church growth.

The Semantics of Success

Paul gives the first-ever church growth seminar in 1 Corinthians 3–4, and his words are as relevant today as then. The apostle defines ministry success, provides a theological vision of church growth, and couches it all in various family metaphors. Leading up to chapter 3, Paul rebukes the personality-cult house churches because a battle is raging among them. He writes, "Now I exhort you, brethren, by the name of our Lord Jesus Christ, that you all agree and that there be no divisions among you, but that you be made complete in the same mind and in the same judgment. For I have been informed concerning you, my brethren, by Chloe's people, that there are quarrels among you. Now I mean this, that each one of you is saying, 'I am of Paul,' and 'I of Apollos,' and 'I of Cephas,' and 'I of Christ'" (1 Cor 1:10–12 NASB). Each house church claimed an apostle or Jesus himself as their leader and argued about who was the best. "I like Paul because he planted our church." "Apollos is the best preacher I've ever heard." "Peter (Cephas) walked on water, something your guy never did." "I'm going to trump you all and play the Jesus card!" Can you imagine the drama in Corinth?

12. Kaiser, *Preaching and Teaching*, 18.

Paul spends most of 1 Corinthians 1–2 defending his ministry style and its apparent lack of success. The apostle isn't eloquent and "wise" like the rhetorically talented sophists the Corinthians hear speaking in the public square each day. The Spirit did not inject Paul with the pizzazz of some teachers. The results of Paul's evangelistic ministry are also unimpressive. Shouldn't more people turn to Christ if Paul is preaching the truth? Yet, according to Paul, the gospel needs no ornamentation because the unbeliever must become captivated by God's grace, not the flair of the messenger. And it's the Spirit's job to convict hearts, not Paul's. This brings us to 1 Corinthians 3.

The Corinthians seem to feel frustrated that they grew very little under Paul's ministry. Paul preached about the death and resurrection of Christ every day, but the church wanted more. A hot new preacher named Apollos came to town. Apollos looked good and had a golden voice, and he was the only reason the Corinthian churches were growing. If Paul reproduced Apollos's methods, all of the apostle's church plants would grow exponentially. Paul disagrees. He would rather serve as a faithful parent than a skilled speaker.

In 1 Corinthians 3:1–3, Paul rebukes his children because they haven't grown up yet. He gave them milk (simplistic teaching) in the beginning because they were infants in Christ. But since then, they have kept fighting like children instead of growing into maturity. Why should Paul feed them steak and potatoes when the Paul-ite and Apollos-ite factions bicker like spoiled toddlers fighting over a toy truck? Paul rebukes Corinth for failing to grow where it matters (in this case, growing in unity) because they're too focused on the wrong kind of growth (growing in the clout brought on by a successful pastor). Paul then gives a brief theology of growth that deserves careful attention.

God, the Grower

First, in 1 Corinthians 3:5, Paul reorients the Corinthians' concept of what a preacher is. "What then is Apollos? And what is Paul? Servants through whom you believed, even as the Lord gave *opportunity* to each one" (NASB, italics original). These men aren't heroes who discovered the hidden keys to successful ministry. Paul and Apollos aren't the reason anyone believed in Christ, any more than a waiter at Red Lobster is the reason the coconut shrimp tastes incredible. The preacher simply brings the message. The Lord alone deserves credit for the beauty of the gospel.

In case the Corinthians didn't get it, Paul goes on. "I planted, Apollos watered, but God was causing the growth. So then neither the one who plants nor the one who waters is anything, but God who causes the growth" (1 Cor 3:6–7 NASB). Paul writes redundantly here because his point is critical. Two things stand out. First, Paul and Apollos—and, by extension, pastors and church leaders today—have a role to play. Paul doesn't act like he contributed nothing to the Corinthian churches. He isn't deterministic about church growth. He doesn't claim, "God is going to do what God is going to do, so don't bother." The minister should do his job, whatever God has assigned. But, all growth, all success, and all credit belong to God alone. This truth must become our sole foundation for a theology of church growth.

Deconstructing the Church Growth Trinity

Let's return for a moment to the three founding values of the modern church growth movement: measurability, reproducibility, and pragmatism. First, church growth gurus demand measurability because any goal that is not numerical is "worthless." By contrast, Paul wants Corinth to grow in one area that is impossible to quantify: unity. Remember that he critiques them for failing to mature, as evidenced by their quarreling. Paul couldn't measure unity, but he knew it when he saw it. And he undoubtedly recognized its absence. He didn't need a bar graph to show him that the churches were fighting (call it qualitative analysis, if that helps). But if Paul ministered according to modern church growth strategies, he would have to focus on quantitative growth he could measure: giving levels or attendance. Even if growth in unity remained in the back of his mind, his efforts would need to concentrate on reaching tangible goals. Such is the problem. Measurability is not unbiblical (Numbers is a book of the Bible), but it can distract the modern minister from values that are biblical, like unity. The pastor can't focus on everything.

Paul also debunks reproducibility, the second church growth value. I won't spend much time on this point, because a simple question will reveal the problem with reproducibility. How can a minister reproduce what only God can produce? Twice, Paul claims that God alone grows the church. Paul also says that human ministers are nothing when it comes to growing the congregation. Paul doesn't equivocate here. Church growth—and I mean real growth, the kind that Paul promotes—is all God, even though the human minister must play his God-given role. God is the sole agent, and we are his instruments. Again, God's sovereignty over church growth does not demand that ministers and members stick their heads in the sand, waiting for God to do whatever he's going to do. As I mentioned in chapter 2, God provides wisdom in all areas of life, even using the business world at times. But the potential for wisdom in the world does not permit us to jettison good theology.

When church growth books address 1 Corinthians 3, they admit that God works behind the scenes, but they also claim that growth strategies equip the minister to play his role most effectively. Yet, reproducibility is the heart of the movement, and it inevitably rips responsibility for growth out of God's hands. So, the church growth movement's theology is not quite as harmless as it seems.

Pragmatism is the third church growth value. To address it, we must continue on in the passage. On the one hand, 1 Corinthians 3:10 (NASB) sounds church growthy when pulled out of context. "According to the grace of God which was given to me, like a wise master builder I laid a foundation, and another is building on it. But each man must be careful how he builds on it." Isn't the goal-setting, number-checking, pattern-studying minister acting like a "wise master builder" who carefully plans his project? Not according to Paul. Goals, numbers, and patterns aren't the materials of a church's foundation. "For no man can lay a foundation other than the one which is laid, which is Jesus Christ" (v. 11 NASB). The careful and wise architect is the one who recognizes that Christ is the only foundation of the church.

Also, an architect should consider his building materials. In verses 12–15, Paul warns that some will build the church with materials that have no eternal value—wood, hay, and straw—while others build with materials that last—gold, silver, and precious stones. Pragmatism says that if you can build a house using wood, hay, and straw, you should. Indeed, modern businesses often aim to create products as cheaply as possible. Jobs travel overseas, metal components become plastic, and quality control is automated, because the means don't matter as much as the bottom line. According to a 2015 Consumer Affairs article, the longest-lasting appliance in a home is a gas range stove, which would have lasted four years longer if you had bought a 1993 model.[13] A business might benefit from the shorter lifespan of its product, but cutting corners doesn't help a church truly grow. Pragmatism risks destroying God's temple—the church—and leaving the foolish builder in a heap of trouble (vv. 15–17).

---

13. Cohen, "Appliances Really Don't Last."

Family Goals

Moving ahead, Paul reiterates in 1 Corinthians 3:18—4:13 that churches should not take pride in their ministers, since everything belongs to God. Paul is a mere servant of the gospel whose only goal is trustworthiness (again, not a measurable outcome). On the other hand, the Corinthians think they deserve credit for their work. But Paul disagrees, writing, "For who regards you as superior? What do you have that you did not receive? And if you did receive it, why do you boast as if you had not received it?" (1 Cor 4:7 NASB). We need these questions today. If churches large and small have been given every good thing by God alone, they have no room for the kind of pride that says, "Look what we did!" A biblical definition of growth destroys pastoral deism.

Finally, Paul returns to a familial analogy as he closes this section in 4:14–21. Notice the familial language in verses 14–17 (NASB), where Paul writes, "I do not write these things to shame you, but to admonish you as my beloved children. For if you were to have countless tutors in Christ, yet you would not have many fathers, for in Christ Jesus I became your father through the gospel. Therefore I exhort you, be imitators of me. For this reason I have sent to you Timothy, who is my beloved and faithful child in the Lord, and he will remind you of my ways which are in Christ, just as I teach everywhere in every church."

Paul, as the Corinthian churches' father, loves them deeply and challenges them to imitate him. Don't picture Paul as a prideful apostle setting himself up as the ultimate example of holiness. Instead, he is a loving father with young children who learn more by watching than by listening. Paul will also send another child, Timothy, while Dad is away to remind the churches of what Paul already said. Otherwise, according to verse 21, Paul might need to come back as a disciplinarian with a rod in hand instead of as a gentle dad.

In all, Paul shows that the solution for bickering, competitive churches is to remember they are a family that only God can grow. No preacher, big or small, can grow a church. Growth is God's work alone. The house churches in Corinth, some of which are increasing in number and fame, cannot attribute their growth to their favorite Christian personality or anything other than what God gave them. They also shouldn't focus on their apparent "success" while they have failed to grow in maturity and unity. Some things matter more than numerical growth and the clout that comes with it. The Corinthians must not only grow but must also (or, even more importantly) mature. And when growth happens, only God deserves the credit.

SWAPPING METAPHORS: REDEFINING GROWTH FOR TODAY

When it comes to church growth, we find ditches on both sides: apathy on one and number-mongering on the other. I think the path is narrower and the ditches wider than many realize. The biblical vision of church growth demands that we carefully define what success looks like today.

Good Growth

The best place to begin is the ubiquitous but vague word *grow*. When someone says, "Our church is growing," most of us hear, "We have more attendees than we used to." Our use of that term must change. I have challenged our pastoral team to use the qualifier *numerical* when talking about increasing attendance. For example, "With this kind of numerical growth, we need to look at adding another service soon." When we begin to distinguish numerical increase from biblical growth, both in our minds and our language, we will make great strides.

We are all a product of our influences. If you start to use the language of *growth* differently, it may result from reading this book and others like it. In the same way, the more church growth material you interact with, the more likely the principles and values of the movement will become your own. For that reason, we must evaluate our influences regularly. Have you accepted church growth principles without considering whether they are theologically accurate? Whether you interact with those who founded the church growth movement (McGavran), expanded it (Rainer and Barna), or have since normalized it (Stanley), be aware of the problematic presuppositions of the movement. Don't presume that measurability, reproducibility, and pragmatism are neutral tools the pastor will always use to the glory of God.

Redefining success also requires an analysis of our ministry priorities. My purpose in this chapter is not to argue that numerical increase is always bad. It could be bad. Church growth gurus love the mantra "Healthy things grow," which is true for a child but less so for an adult. I'm in my mid-thirties, and if part of me is growing, it's probably my belly. Worse yet, as Jared Wilson puts it, "Healthy things grow, but so does cancer."[14] Some of the largest churches have tumors of poor theology and dissension popping up all over. Still, my point is not that big is bad but, rather, that big isn't our priority.

Numerical data can help us make wise decisions, or it can hurt. Statistics can be to the pastor's ego what a liquor store is to the recovering

14. Wilson, *Prodigal Church*, 40.

alcoholic. Data carries an intrinsic risk. Numbers can inflate the pride of "successful" pastors and kill the joy of others. Look at this testimony from Simon Murphy, a successful church planter by most measures:

> My church plant success didn't preclude me from needing to walk by faith. And when my faith faltered, I resorted to self-reliance which proved to be highly destructive. Self-reliance is a cancerous presence that eats its own host as it struggles for survival. We "dig deep" to do what needs to be done. It's a socially acceptable sin, and often encouraged in church planters because it masquerades as faithfulness, diligence, and hard work. These qualities are all commendable. But beneath these external actions could well be a denial of the Fatherly care of God, and a disbelief in Jesus' promise that He will build His church.[15]

I fear that pastors might gain what they've always wanted and, at the same time, find themselves further from God than they've ever been. On the other hand, when we prioritize the kind of growth that only God can bring—faith, righteousness, hope, kindness, unity, and so on—we'll find that real church growth provokes worship in us, not pride.

Putting Pastors in Their Places

A related point concerns the tendency to treat pastors like celebrities. I am confident pastors would be healthier in every way if we treated them like siblings and not like supermen. Because I like to eavesdrop on the conversations of my students before class, I recently heard a student gushing about the time she met a megachurch pastor while overseas. By her own account, she nearly fainted and, though remaining conscious, stumbled over her words like a starstruck thirteen-year-old. Meeting this preacher ranks as one of the greatest moments of her life, she claimed. And this college student is not alone.

Students frequently discuss which celebrity pastors will preach at a given conference to determine if it's worth attending. They spout off the quotes of these men as if Jesus himself said their words. The whole thing scares me. These men are successful in many ways, and most are admirably faithful to the Lord. But any success these pastors experienced, any growth that has mattered, came from the Lord. I believe most of these men would tell my students not to exalt them. Still, we risk worshiping the man and not his God. This is sinful. We must confess the ease with which we idolize

---

15. Murphy, "I Was a Successful Church Planter."

people who, according to Paul, are nobodies (myself included). I am concerned that we have practiced this sin to the point that we no longer recognize it as sin. May God forgive us.

Plant and Water vs. Copy and Paste

In addition to confessing our idolatry, let's also lay aside the temptation to reproduce what megachurches have done. The copy and paste approach to church growth is lazy at best and cuts God out of the process at worst. Instead, we must beg God for real growth and then plant and water where he leads. If 1 Corinthians 3 is any indication, you can't grow the church, but you can tear it down (1 Cor 3:17). So, work hard to protect the church and to serve faithfully, all the while praying that God will bring real growth.

Paul prioritizes relationships when discussing growth. Does your church? Are your resources targeted at increasing attendance only? I recommend auditing your church's schedule to determine where, if anywhere, the church provides opportunities for believers to know the sins and successes in one another's lives. I believe churches of all sizes need small group ministries that facilitate discussions about the daily lives of each participant. Each group member admits what has been draining them emotionally, physically, and spiritually, and they rejoice over what God has used to fill them up lately. Prayer and daily encouragement become the primary tools of small group members. I also recommend a separate Bible study or Sunday School ministry that allows smaller groups to study Scripture collectively in a way that looks more like 1 Corinthians 14. By separating Bible study classes from small groups, we allow time for two distinct but central aspects of church life. When we add in worship services, we create a trinity of gathering opportunities to shape a group of disconnected believers into a spiritually and relationally deep church family.

A local church should pursue spiritual health and unity within the church family, but we cannot lose sight of evangelism. Recall that numerical growth in Acts is directly linked with gospel proclamation or the direct work of the Spirit. Luke describes no goal-setting session at the first ministry conference. The church of Antioch probably didn't study how the Jerusalem church reached people, hoping to reproduce their methods. So why should our church strategy sessions focus on what other churches are doing to increase attendance? Instead of worrying about the church down the road, let's brainstorm ways we might encourage believers to start gospel conversations with non-believers in their unique workplaces. We can preach about the beauty of salvation. We can offer simple evangelistic tools to calm the nerves of anxious witnesses. And we can remind people that the Spirit does the hardest work when we present the gospel of Jesus.[16]

Finally, remember that Paul sprinkled family language (*brethren*) throughout 1 Corinthians 3–4. "And I, brethren, could not speak to you as to spiritual men, but as to men of flesh, as to infants in Christ" (3:1 NASB). He could have called them dumb or unskilled workers, but he chose to picture them as his children. In the same way, Paul writes, "Now these things, brethren, I have figuratively applied to myself and Apollos for your sakes, so that in us you may learn not to exceed what is written, so that no one of you will become arrogant in behalf of one against the other" (4:6 NASB). When he rebukes their disunity, Paul reminds the Corinthians that they are family. Churches fighting over whose celebrity pastor is the greatest must remember that the church is a family with only one Father. Church families might fight, just as biological families do. But they fight with love and resolve conflict with forgiveness. Because fighting well protects church members from hurting one another, we turn to the subject of conflict in the next chapter.

16. For a helpful list of questions for analyzing real growth, see Wilson, *Prodigal Church*, 158.

6

Fighting against Division, Not One Another

The Biblical Response to Conflict

Successfully growing a loyal church attendance is similar to growing a loyal customer base for any form of business or brand, and it involves a *clear* brand marketing strategy.

—CHURCHBRANDGUIDE.COM

I AM EMBARRASSED TO admit that the seasons of ministry I most dreaded as a vocational pastor were Christmas and Easter. My primary tasks were planning Sunday services and executing every component except preaching (although that role grew later in my ministry). I created videos, song lyric slides, chord charts for musicians, and set lists for all involved. On Sundays, I was part worship leader and part tour guide, leading congregants on the journey that was our worship service. I wonder how often I have told people to stand or sit throughout my years as a worship pastor. One Sunday, I told the congregation to face the back of the church, only because I wanted to see if they would comply. And they did! I was their Siri, and they would have driven into a lake if I had instructed them to do so.

God blessed me with an excellent worship band, and I felt that we met or exceeded the average person's expectations most Sundays. That is, until one of the big holidays arrived. I don't recall any pastor or church member sitting me down and saying, "Matt, this is the last Sunday before Christmas. We need pyrotechnics, surprise celebrity appearances, tear-jerking videos, and the Spirit to fall like a rainstorm in April." But I put the weight of everyone's unspoken expectations on my shoulders. Inevitably, someone would send me a video of a hipster church band playing "Rudolph the Red-Nosed Reindeer," using equipment from the Guitar Hero video game. And the weight of expectations would increase. Another church family praised a neighboring church's carefully choreographed choir who belted classic Easter hymns. And the weight would increase. I would see billboards advertising the megachurch's Christmas Spectacular, and the weight would increase. Worst of all, I would hear about a church member's plan to "experience" a different church on Easter Sunday, and the weight would nearly crush me.

What motivated this spirit of competition? Sometimes, my insecurity motivated me. Imposter syndrome would rear its ugly head when I feared church members might recognize that I had "faked it until I made it" but that I didn't really know how to do my job. On the other hand, pride motivated me when I simply wanted to be better than Third Baptist Church down the road. Most often, though, I simply longed to meet the grandiose expectations I assumed our church members held when a holiday drew near. My job was to fulfill each individual's hopes and dreams of what a Christmas service could be, right? Otherwise, what if they attended another church's "experience" and became infatuated with their brand? In the end, I believed my obligation was to keep our customers happy. I drank the Christian consumerism Kool-Aid without realizing it. Yet, as dangerous as my perspective was as a pastor, a consumeristic mindset is even more dangerous for the church member.

IF THE CHURCH IS A BUSINESS:
THE BASIS OF DIVISION

For immunocompromised individuals, the body's defense system begins at a weakened state. Viruses and infections that the typical immune system could ward off pose lethal threats to the immunocompromised. Take COVID-19, for example. This one virus could impact two people differently based on their prior immune stability. Those who began in a weakened condition were more likely to face serious, even deadly, complications from COVID.

The same risk applies to the church, whose collective immune system is weakened by consumerism, especially when trying to fight division. Although a solitary conflict may not threaten the average church, those operating with a consumeristic perspective risk losing members—hands, feet, and everything in between—at an increased rate. This weakened immune system in a consumeristic church has little to no ability to fight one of the most pervasive infections to any church body: division. Before we explain why consumerism presents such a risk to church health during conflict, let's consider the causes of church fights.

Realizing We're Naked

I wish I could believe the optimistic views of human nature espoused in pop culture. Humans are basically good. Evil is an anomaly. I can be better. I would relish such wishful thinking if Genesis 3 didn't tell a different story.

As we read about the fall of humanity, we might not expect that the first two consequences of sin in Genesis 3 harm human relationships. First, the woman gives the fruit to her husband. I don't possess the skills needed to psychoanalyze Eve, but experience tells me that sinners often want others to join in their sin. Romans 1 ends by warning that those who devolve into a cycle of sin eventually applaud the debauchery of their fellow sinners. Paul writes in Rom 1:32 (NASB), "And although they know the ordinance of God, that those who practice such things are worthy of death, they not only do the same, but also approve of those who practice them." Misery loves company, and so does sin. If you don't believe me, watch videos of parents putting their young children through the moral gauntlet known as the Fruit Snack Challenge. The parent places a fruit snack, cookie, or bowl of candy in front of a toddler and tells the child not to touch it until the parent returns. Mom and Dad then leave the room to generate years of future counseling fodder for the toddler. My favorite version is when multiple kids face the challenge at the same time. Inevitably, one toddler caves. The impulsive child then either eats everyone else's candy or tells the others to join in. "After all," the little one must think, "I ate it, and nothing bad happened."

The tendency to encourage others to join our sin began with Eve, but it continues today when conflict divides a congregation. In the book *Firestorm*, Ron Susek describes multiple phases that lead to a fiery church split. After the sparks of conflict lead to small relational fires, opposing perspectives harden into distinct parties with leaders and representatives on each side.[1] It's us versus them. Attempts at Christ-like behavior disappear as mobs form, spurred on by a shared desire to defeat the sinners on the other side. We may put lipstick on our side's slanderous words by describing them in godly categories—calling out sin, defending truth, etc.—but we're just like Eve. We're eating the forbidden fruit and passing it along to those closest to us. "Eat it," we say. "Slander tastes great!" Our Facebook likes and posts show that we "approve of those who practice" slander.

Adam eats the fruit without recorded comment, leading to the second consequence of sin. The couple realizes they're naked. I know this sounds odd to modern ears and even stranger to Westerners surrounded by a sexually confused society. But before the first sin, Genesis 2 records a vow-like marriage covenant, "At last this is bone of my bones, and flesh of my flesh" (v. 23 NASB), and then comments, "And the man and his wife were both naked, but they were not ashamed" (v. 25 NASB). Quite literally, Adam and Eve knew no boundaries. No relational walls existed. Not until sin stole their innocence.

The Apples Haven't Fallen Far

Christians battle one another, because sin builds walls between people, just as it did between Adam and Eve. The plants the first couple used to shield themselves became the first literal relational barrier in human history but certainly not the last. By Genesis 4, the relational break in humanity leads to the first murder, not the murder of a threatening stranger but a godly brother. Cain kills his brother out of jealousy due to Abel's act of worship, launching the first worship war in human history. Since that time, the apples haven't fallen far from the tree.

The pages that follow in Scripture reveal a downward spiral among human relationships, all of which began with the first couple's sense of shame. As we consider the source of church conflict, we see that Adam and Eve's shame means that humans no longer know one another fully and that self-preservation (in their case, hiding) supersedes relational oneness. We prefer to hide and protect ourselves rather than open up to others. And with Cain, we easily allow secret suspicions to mutate into relationally violent behavior. Little has changed since Genesis 3–4.

Scripture teaches us that sin draws the battle lines between humans, even between Christian siblings. Maybe this seems too obvious, but the implications are significant. "That person" is not the root of your conflict. Sin is. And if sin is the root problem, our solutions must defeat sin's hold.

1. Susek, *Firestorm*, 46.

For example, removing that person from your life doesn't necessarily satisfy the end goal of vanquishing sin. The only lasting solution is gospel-rooted forgiveness.

Responding to Offense

A related implication of Genesis 3–4 is that my sinful flesh will always make the conflict worse, even when I'm the victim. To be clear, I do not mean the victim caused the conflict or bears any blame for being victimized—not at all. What I mean is that I will respond to an attack, whether a serious one that deserves a legal response or merely feeling ignored by the small group leader, with actions tinged by my sinful flesh. Whether I am tempted to fight or fly when wronged, I must run my response through a gospel filter to prevent a deeper divide from forming. And the gospel always prioritizes reconciliation over vengeance or even relational separation.[2] The Band-Aid of chewing out our opponent or avoiding the church loudmouth won't suffice, because such responses don't address the heart issues at play. Quick fixes risk stitching up a wound with a raging infection still inside. The church consumer, however, won't see it that way.

We once had a bad experience at a local restaurant. Forty minutes after ordering, our food hadn't arrived. Normally, I would grow frustrated but would wait it out due to sheer laziness, if nothing else. On this fateful day, however, the slow service meant we would be running late for a funeral (for the record, my wife warned me we wouldn't have enough time). When we politely asked the staff to box up our food rather than bring it to the table, one waitress loudly criticized our ignorance. "Don't they know our food is homemade? How long do they think it takes to cook from scratch?" We had ordered eggs and pancakes, by the way, so I didn't think the cook needed much time to make it from scratch. After experiencing abysmal service and yucky food, my wife and I made a pact not to step foot in that restaurant again. And that's okay, because we're just customers. But avoidance can't be our response to offensive siblings in the church. The family deserves better.

Church consumers won't hesitate to withdraw from Christian community. They'll take flight at the first offense and feel vindicated, even righteous, in doing so. And in a church surrounded by other humans undergoing the

---

2. In the case of abuse, however, the only right solution is to remove the abused person from the situation immediately. The healing process, often including serious repercussions for the abuser, can begin only once everyone's safety is ensured. And because we will not fully defeat sin in this life, those who are abused usually need to establish clear relational boundaries for future protection.

painful process of sanctification, it doesn't take long to feel offended. But withdrawing doesn't resolve the conflict. It doesn't hold the offender responsible or seek reconciliation. It doesn't overlook the sinful action in light of the debt Christ forgave in my life. Withdrawing is a poor substitute for healing, just as hiding behind some foliage was a weak solution for Adam and Eve. Breaking contact may be a proper response for a frustrated consumer, but it isn't how brothers and sisters should live.

The Social Media Monster

Let's pause and imagine a world where local churches are havens of peace and forgiveness. We would confront sin with undeniable love and overlook minor wrongs, all while submitting to the preferences of others for the sake of unity. News agencies would report the surprising flood of affection displayed at denominational meetings. Unbelievers would flock to this relational oasis in the desert of war and violence. In a word, it would be heaven.

Our reality, unfortunately, is that sin continues to infect the lives of believers. Consequently, church conflict remains inevitable. Even the earliest churches fought (see 1 Cor 1:11; 3:3; Phil 1:15–17; Titus 3:9–11). But some unique aspects of modern life make resolving conflict more difficult than what the early Christians faced. Among our most daunting challenges is social media.

Social media could energize evangelism by removing the travel costs and national borders that have hindered global missions for centuries. A few taps on a screen could fling doors to the gospel wide open in regions of the world where travel is difficult. Although I haven't seen evidence of a great revival sparked by social media, I hope some witness God working in this way.

Social media is a tool designed to make private communication public, to amplify our whispers through a digital megaphone the whole world can hear. The problem is that few messages deserve such a massive audience. If social media can broadcast our gospel witness, it can also amplify criticism, in-fighting, and suspicion. Imagine if the first-century "super-apostles" polluting the Corinthian congregation (2 Cor 11:1–6) had held sway over a million Twitter followers. They could have run Paul's ministry into the mud, not only in Greece but also in Rome, Ephesus, Antioch, and even Jerusalem, with the click of a button. Today, a lone critic can (rightly or wrongly) build a coalition of supporters and topple long-standing institutions and individuals in a matter of weeks. The online court of public opinion now tramples thoughtful, compassionate debate like a tank in a corn field. And we Christians seem just as willing as unbelievers to use this weapon of mass destruction against our brothers and sisters.[3]

The Root of Consumerism

How could we possibly excuse our willingness to destroy Christian siblings? I suggest that Christian consumerism is a major contributor, because it breeds pride and selfishness. By Christian consumerism, I refer to the perspective that the church exists for my benefit. The Christian consumer *shops* for a church based on his preferred style of music, preaching, and programs. He *volunteers* when convenient in order to feel good.[4] He regards fellow believers as servants of his own needs or, as I often feel at the grocery store, as objects in his way. If he steps into leadership, he sees other churches as competition, maybe even as enemies. He will attack those who deny his preferences and mock members whose desires differ from his. In short, the Christian consumer's focus is himself.

Few of us are willing to face our consumeristic tendencies with eyes wide open, but researchers have begun to shine a light on the trends. Jim Van Yperen runs a church reconciliation company called Metanoia Ministries. In his book, *Making Peace*, Van Yperen notes, "Of the more than 5,000 people we have interviewed during the past eight years, in traditional as well as contemporary churches, most believers evaluate their church positively or negatively in consumer, transactional terms. Christians choose a church for the same inclinations and motivations that they choose a supermarket."[5] Many Western Christians treat church programming like a buffet. I'll take the youth ministry from First Baptist, the music at Graceline, and the small groups organized by Lifeblood Church. Why do some Christians sample churches like hors d'oeuvres, while other believers show up as often as they go to the dentist? Because consumers are no longer satisfied with the options available at traditional churches.[6] In other words, churches are no longer meeting their desires.

I imagine that most readers, especially pastors, affirm my lament over these trends. But, leaders, we are living in the house we've been building

---

3. If you need evidence, look back through the Twitter discussions between Southern Baptists around the time of the 2021 annual meeting in Nashville.

4. If the church is a family, the language of volunteering doesn't work, for the same reason that I don't call mowing my lawn volunteer work. Volunteering implies working without obligation.

5. Van Yperen, *Making Peace*, 33.

6. Jethani, *Immeasurable*, 164.

for decades. We should expect consumeristic attendees when our structures and priorities scream, "The church is a business!" Our congregations are following our lead. Think about the recent proliferation of books and businesses providing marketing strategies for churches. One website offers a five-step plan that promises "the transformation of potential customers, or 'strangers,' into fully loyal and dedicated church members, or 'champions.'"[7] Another site describes the gospel as the "product" Christians sell.[8] We cannot sell the gospel to church customers and then expect them to drop their consumeristic mindsets and act like selfless siblings under the fatherhood of God. Whatever root metaphor we build into our church life will shape the habits of our people. So, if the church is a business, expect believers to act like consumers.

The Black Friday Mentality

Church conflict is a natural byproduct of Christian consumerism. Van Yperen draws the connection, writing, "A church organized around meeting needs breeds selfishness, and it inevitably leads to competition, control, and conflict."[9] Compare marital conflict. A husband and wife don't usually fight because they passionately prioritize the other person's preferences. Instead, they each fight for their own desires. In the same way, consumerism celebrates the perspective that my desires matter most, not yours. If you feel the same way about your preferences, then we may hold hands in ministry only as long as our desires align. But the moment our preferences diverge, those hands will become fists.

Following the glorious day Walmart introduced the curbside pickup, I have spent little time in brick-and-mortar stores. But for decades of my life, I actually bought products inside the store like it was the 1800s. And what I remember is that nothing exciting happened except on one day each year: Black Friday.

In the era before we could shop for Black Friday deals online, we would wait outside in the cold morning hours on the day after Thanksgiving to save three dollars on some high thread-count bedsheets. When you entered Wally World early on Friday morning, it was like an apocalyptic bomb had gone off inside the store. At some unknown hour, the employees had rearranged the store and built mountains of discounted products in the middle of the aisles. They had designed new pathways using caution

7. Persaud, "Creating Clear Church Marketing Strategy."
8. "Four P's of Church Marketing."
9. Van Yperen, *Making Peace*, 35.

tape and empty shelving. And everyone had gone insane. I saw seemingly ordinary people screaming at strangers over cutting in line. Some customers hoarded the most highly discounted items to sell them with a 200 percent mark-up to the chumps who didn't wake up early enough. People who usually shopped together amiably—when their interests aligned—accessed the depths of their sin nature when TVs went on sale for a few hours on a cold Friday morning.

Similar events happen in churches. Most infamous are the worship wars between the traditional and contemporary camps. Christian siblings who weep together over lost friends one week turn on each other the next over the inclusion of drums in the worship set. Why? Because their desires no longer align. Both long for the salvation of the lost, just as average Walmart shoppers want an orderly, humane shopping experience. But when two believers face the possibility that their own musical preferences might be denied, Sunday morning can quickly turn into Black Friday.

The Black Friday mentality can invade church staff as well. Why do the youth pastor and women's minister try to undermine each other's ministries when budgeting season rolls around? Because their interests no longer align, making them competitors for those precious budget dollars. I led the youth worship band on Wednesday nights when I was sixteen years old, and I can remember a college leader reprimanding me for laying their ministry's rugs on the stage we shared, because those rugs were for Sunday morning only. So, whether the breaking point is practical or theological, trivial or essential, Christian consumers who disagree are willing to tear one another apart in personal conversations and on social media when their interests diverge.

Beyond budget battles and worship wars are the daily spats that result from personality differences. For example, when our family faces trauma, we prefer our Christian siblings to text us or send cards rather than call and pelt us with questions. But I know other brothers and sisters who feel offended when I don't call immediately after tragedy strikes. Neither preference is better or worse, and the Bible condemns neither. Many tastes come from our uniqueness as humans. Conflict, though, can arise from these minor differences and eventually destroy Christian communities infected by consumerism. If I allow my individualism to go unchecked, I will sacrifice the group on the altar of my desires.

The immunocompromised consumeristic church will struggle even in the face of trivial disagreements. All parties will seek to fulfill their own desires, leaving no one to put the family's collective health first. Conflict rooted in consumerism destroys the joy of church life and sullies the gospel message. In John 13:35 (NASB), Jesus tells his disciples, "By this all men will know that you are My disciples, if you have love for one another." Restated negatively, no one will know you are my disciples if you tear one another apart. Conflict is inevitable, but our response to infighting matters more than we may realize.

IF THE CHURCH IS A FAMILY: A BETTER WAY TO BATTLE

Since the church's inception, one of the enemy's most devastating tools has been disunity within the family of God. Consequently, the New Testament authors respond to disunity in passage after passage, but none gives a more concise solution than Paul in Philippians 2:3–4. Paul writes, "Do nothing from selfishness or empty conceit, but with humility consider one another as more important than yourselves; do not merely look out for your own personal interests, but also for the interests of others." Paul then looks to the exemplary suffering and exaltation of Jesus as the gospel-rooted motivation for the Philippian church's selfless behavior.

Any lasting solution to disunity must begin with the gospel. Without faith in the sacrificial death of Jesus, sin will rule every behavior and attitude. On the other hand, the salvation God freely offers empowers the believer who seeks to live as a Christ-like servant by the power of the Holy Spirit. Only through a relationship with a foot-washing, outcast-loving, cross-bearing Savior can we begin to "consider one another as more important than yourselves" and exalt "the interests of others." The only antidote to self-centered living is Jesus.

The gospel comes first, but years of church life have surgically removed my naïvety bone. The beauty of the gospel is its simplicity—by grace, through faith for all who believe. Spiritual growth (*sanctification*) isn't quite as simple. If it were, we probably wouldn't need most of the New Testament's pleas to live out the gospel in the entirety of our lives. We could also gloss over the many examples of how to apply the gospel in specific situations.

Of course, the New Testament is an ancient document, so not every instruction and example directly matches our modern experiences. Take, for example, the issue of meat sacrificed to idols in 1 Corinthians 8–10 or the subject of head coverings and hair length in chapter 11. Most of us don't worry about how trips to the supermarket or the barber impact our church. Other situations, though, require little modern imagination, because they align so closely with our struggles. Paul confronts one such case in 1 Corinthians 6:1–8, a passage that also emphasizes the siblingship of believers.

To Sue or Not to Sue

In 1 Corinthians 6, Paul criticizes the Corinthian believers for suing one another and offers an obvious solution: "Don't take one another to court!" We may think Paul's zeal got the best of him. Do lawsuits really matter? Does Paul mean to be so absolute in his prohibition? If we look at the situation with ancient eyes, we may better recognize why Paul so aggressively opposes Christian versus Christian lawsuits.

The legal process in a Roman province like Achaia (a region that included Athens and Corinth) looked like a hybrid between Judge Judy and the tribal council on an episode of Survivor. Disputes about money and property fell upon local magistrates who, in essence, had the freedom to shape local laws as they saw fit. When a new magistrate came into power in Rome, he would publish his own principles and standards by which he would judge cases.[10] Clearly, consistency wasn't a top priority.

One common standard that did not need formal publication was "might makes right." Court spectators anticipated that the person with higher social status or the means to offer an attractive bribe would win the day, making the case's arguments moot.[11] Because of the influence of the mighty, the legal system failed to enact what the Bible would call justice. The rich and powerful defeated their inferiors with few exceptions.

Despite the broken legal system, people continued to sue each other. And in a time when few options for free entertainment existed, trials became a spectator sport for the masses. Think of it as a precursor to the John Grisham novel. Rhetorically gifted lawyers like Cicero gained celebrity status with their quick wit and sharp tongues. Even in boring civil suits, rhetorical flare played a role as important as any evidence.

Much like modern political debates, one common strategy was to attack your opponent's character.[12] Convince everyone he is a lowlife, and you will win the case. Imagine two believers fighting over money before a pagan judge and a jury of the city elite. One believer publicly proclaims that his Christian brother is a charlatan who cheats and lies, because he doesn't possess the intelligence to make an honest profit. The other believer responds—again, publicly—that his freeloading fool of an opponent refuses to pay a fair price, because he squanders his meager income at the local brothel every night. After only a few cases, the audience would learn that

---

10. Jeffers, *Greco-Roman World*, 155.

11. Winter, "Civil Litigation in Secular Corinth," 564–66.

12. Winter, "Civil Litigation in Secular Corinth," 564–66.

Christians acted no differently than any other wronged person. Now, maybe we can better understand Paul's concern.

A Better Way for Believers

In 1 Corinthians 6:1–8, Paul follows his instructions on judging sin within the church (1 Cor 5) with a litany of questions that would make the best trial lawyer blush. "Do you dare to go to public court? Aren't you destined to exercise judgment on a grander scale? Is there no one sensible enough among you to mediate these minor issues?"[13] I imagine that when the letter was read in each Corinthian house church, those gathered squirmed like scolded children.

Paul's sharp rebuke gives two responses to personal conflicts in the church: a *better* approach and the *best* one. Better than taking one another to court would be to mediate disputes internally. In verse 1, Paul reprimands believers for seeking judges among the "unrighteous" rather than the "saints." Those familiar with churchy language will immediately think of righteousness in spiritual terms, but Paul's language would also describe someone who doesn't judge fairly. I joke with my daughter that she can't win in a dispute with her little brother, because my wife and I, the family judges, are both the babies of our families. We will defend the younger child because we identify with his plight. If that were true (most of the time, it isn't), we would be "unrighteous" judges. Paul's first question asks why the Corinthian church members would appeal to a judge who doesn't rule justly. Why not trust the saints—the holy, set apart people of God—to dispense true justice?

In verses 2–3, Paul travels back to the future to show that God's people possess the competence to rule and judge righteously. The strangeness of Paul's claims about Christians judging the world and even angels at the end of time deserves exploration, but our focus here is the big picture. Believers will join Christ in ruling and judging creation, as God designed humans to do from the beginning.[14] If God has prepared such a critical role for the saints, why do the Corinthians act like they can't assess minor disagreements within the body? A Supreme Court justice who returns home for the evening is undoubtedly qualified to determine which of her children ate the missing Snickers bar. Likewise, the Corinthians possess the God-given capacity to judge and, thus, to settle their own conflicts.

---

13. Author's paraphrase.

14. See Gen 2:15; Ps 8; Dan 7:22. Schreiner, *First Corinthians*, 118–19, emphasizes Christians governing at the end of time rather than litigating per se.

Paul moves in verses 5–6 from logic to emotion, shaming his audience for their foolish decisions. Although Paul's sharp critique stands on its own, we must turn back a few pages to feel the full effect. From the beginning of 1 Corinthians, Paul plays off of the wise versus fool dichotomy, almost certainly because the Corinthian church prized Greek wisdom (especially rhetoric and philosophy). Being so close to Athens, the Corinthians likely idolized certain sages who lived like local celebrities. Paul, however, doesn't present his message like a sage. As we mentioned in a previous chapter, Paul refused to make the gospel palatable to their elitist sensibilities by employing fancy rhetorical flourishes and complicated philosophical schemes. For example, in 1 Corinthians 3:18 (NASB), he writes, "Let no man deceive himself. If any man among you thinks that he is wise in this age, he must become foolish, so that he may become wise." The apparent paradox implies that gospel *foolishness* is the only true wisdom available.

Returning to the issue of lawsuits in 6:5–6, we notice that Paul's incredulous question mocks the Corinthians' self-perception. "Is there no one wise enough to mediate these conflicts?" Can't you wise guys figure out basic conflict mediation? Behind Paul's sarcasm is a legitimate concern that the Corinthians remain stuck in their old ways. Why would people who believe in their own wisdom continue to frequent the law court? Most likely, they sue one another because they always have. "That's the way we've always done it," they thought (and were not the last church to do so). Maybe no one had suggested a better way until Paul wrote these words. Or, the Corinthians might have ignored Paul's foolish wisdom in favor of what everyone else does. Either way, their habits needed to change.

Paul does not unpack why lawsuits between Christian siblings are so harmful, but he does place a noteworthy word at a point of emphasis, ending the paragraph with the term *unbeliever*. At this point in the argument, Paul focuses on the spiritual state of those witnessing brothers tear one another down. Paul expressed a similar concern for outsiders when he chastised the church's acceptance of gross sexual sin in the congregation, lamenting that even the gentiles don't tolerate such actions (1 Cor 5:1). In both cases, the church's collective witness faces irreparable harm if believers fail to address sin in godly ways. Unbelievers are watching closely.

The Best Way for Believers

Although taking disputes before the church is better than going to the pagan courts, Paul moves on to a third option—the best way. No matter who mediates a conflict, "it is already a defeat for you," Paul claims in verse 7 (NASB).

Once again, Paul writes concisely, but the introduction of sibling language in verse 5 gives us clues about his reasoning.

Despite the ancient world's emphasis on sibling affection, lawsuits between brothers were common when it came time to divide the family inheritance. Students training in the art of public speaking practiced with case studies about brothers fighting over money.[15] Many of these standardized situations resemble Jesus's parable of the prodigal son, where a reliable son begins to hate his rebellious brother. The ancient case studies (and common sense) also reveal that lawsuits did little to restore fondness between siblings. Thus, the defeat Paul has in mind at this point in his argument does not refer to the Corinthians' gospel witness, which shouldn't suffer if the quarrel remains in-house. Instead, Paul worries about the relationship between siblings who choose any type of litigation, even before Christian judges.

Paul's shocking solution to church conflict is "get over it." Accept that you have been wronged, and move on. I wonder if the Corinthian house churches drew in sharp breaths when they heard Paul's questions read. "Why not rather be wronged? Why not rather be defrauded?" (1 Cor 6:7b NASB). I would want to shout out, "Because it isn't fair!" If you have ever witnessed injustice, you may have felt the knot that forms deep in your gut when you watch someone suffer and know you can't overturn the wrong. I hate waiting and hoping justice will prevail. I want microwave justice. But God is much more patient than I am.

Although he doesn't say it here, we can look to Paul's theology of justice in Romans 12 to understand the apostle's thinking. After discussing brotherly love (12:10) and sharing one mind as a church (12:16), Paul urges in verses 18–19 (NIV), "If it is possible, as far as it depends on you, live at peace with everyone. Do not take revenge, my dear friends, but leave room for God's wrath, for it is written: 'It is mine to avenge; I will repay,' says the Lord." Paul leaves no room for microwave justice—which usually means immediate revenge—because punishment is God's prerogative. My job is peace. God's job, and his alone, is punishment. Peter articulates a similar view when talking about Jesus's exemplary suffering. First Peter 2:23 (NASB) says, "And while being reviled, He did not revile in return; while suffering, He uttered no threats, but kept entrusting Himself to Him who judges righteously." If Jesus can wait patiently for God to enact justice even though he, of all people, did not deserve the violence done to him, can't the Christian who was wronged by a brother avoid litigation and wait on God?

---

15. Peppard, "Brother against Brother."

The Court of Public Opinion

When it comes to Christian conflict today, everything has changed, and nothing has changed. The American legal system is woefully imperfect, but I will take it any day over the kangaroo court in first-century Corinth. Our appeals procedures, commitment to due process, and presumption of innocence provide at least some protections for those wrongfully accused. Our laws are more consistent. We no longer whip people before they give their testimonies in hopes of beating honest answers out of them. So, much has changed.

Yet, Paul's instructions apply today, because the risks remain the same. Beyond court TV, most people don't watch real court cases for entertainment, but Christian legal battles remain as public as ever. Many legal proceedings are published online so that the average citizen or reporter can find the nitty-gritty details after a few minutes on Google. Formal legal decisions are difficult to hide.

But court cases aren't the church's only problem. Even our internal battles garner national media attention, with most news agencies eager to paint our spats in the most dramatic and worst light possible. Like never before, the world is watching how we handle disputes, and I fear that few know we are Christ-followers by our love.

And then there's Twitter. In June 2021, the *Los Angeles Times* devoted a story to the Southern Baptist Convention's annual meeting in Nashville. The article cited an SBC seminary professor's admission that the denomination was seeing historic levels of "polarization and conflict." The journalist devoted ink to a former SBC leader's leaked letter that lamented "blatant, gutter-level racism . . . behind closed doors." The author also noted the "wave of conservatives [who] took to Twitter" before the meeting.[16] This line is significant, because the journalist did not gain the information from a press release or phone interview but from perusing social media. My point is that when our internal squabbles play out on social media—and they do, often—the watching world gains a permanent record of our fleshly behavior. I attended the annual meeting and left pleased by the way most conducted themselves in person. But online, many of my fellow Great Commission Baptists actively destroyed our witness to the unbelieving world. The irony truly pains me.

Why then are we boldly displaying our dirty laundry online? After all, we are not blind to the negative impact of our social media tantrums. From what I have seen, though, social media crusaders blast other believers to

---

16. Jarvie, "Averting an Ultraconservative Takeover."

sway the court of public opinion. The idea is simple. If people see and hear an idea often enough, they will begin to believe it. I could start a campaign that says the president is an alien from Mars. If I can build a large and passionate coalition to spread this silly claim, people will begin to wonder if it might be true. In the Christian world, the claim may be that Bob is a heretic, Lisa is a closet liberal, or Jim is running the organization into the ground.[17] The claims may or may not prove accurate. But the evidence is irrelevant when the court of public opinion comes into play.

But Paul won't allow the Corinthians to arbitrate their disagreements in the court of public opinion. And the modern court of public opinion is as unjust as a pagan magistrate. It harms our witness as much as personal attacks before an ancient judge and jury. And it divides siblings in Christ as much as constant litigation inside or outside the Corinthian courts.

Family-Style Conflict

How then do we apply 1 Corinthians 6:1–8 today? I suggest we treat all Christian siblings the same way we strive to treat the family members living in our household, or at least how we know we should treat them. Doing so would correspond to the expectations Jesus articulates in Matthew 18. For example, I have been in pastoral ministry long enough to know that a high percentage of married couples in a congregation are fighting at any given moment. Yet, with few exceptions, I don't see husbands and wives criticizing one another on Facebook. They keep their digital mouths shut, because they know better. You don't publicly attack your wife if you are trying to heal the relationship. You talk directly to her with honesty and understanding, and you take steps to reconcile.

Most of us protect our kids online, too. Some of us share funny stories of mistakes our kids have made or silly conflicts we have resolved. But even in my preaching, I try not to tell a story that would embarrass my children now or later. I know that once my words leave my mouth, I can't take them back.

A family should also desire to walk in forgiveness. Sometimes, forgiveness requires confrontation so that the relationship can improve. But, following Paul's advice, we can overlook perceived wrongs, giving the person the benefit of the doubt ("They're just tired" is a common claim in our household). We need the wisdom to know when to tell our children to pick up their smelly shoes for the fifth time and when to do the work ourselves.

17. See, for example, this unfortunate recent battle in Roach, "Platt's McLean Bible Church."

Do they need a loving lesson or an act of grace? For relatively healthy families, either response to conflict should come naturally.

Now comes the big ask. I think we must stop using social media to share our critiques, concerns, and frustrations about other believers and Christian institutions. Yes, I know that will cut the number of posts by half (and we could eliminate social media altogether if our kids stop being cute). But, I think this is a realistic and necessary application of what the Bible says. If we agree with Paul that our gospel witness and Christian unity matter greatly, then let me paraphrase one of my mom's favorite proverbs: "If you can't think of something kind to say, don't say anything."[18]

Maybe you're thinking, "But how will I get the word out that she is doing the wrong thing?" If that's you, please realize your sentiment appeals to the court of public opinion and is the exact opposite of what Jesus commanded in Matthew 18. In other words, your natural inclination is to begin the reconciliation process at the final step: tell it to the church (and, at the same time, the lost world!). Instead, you should start with the first step and talk to your sibling about your concerns. If that sibling is someone with whom you don't have a personal relationship or to whom you can't gain access, then maybe you are not the person God has appointed to confront the problem. Perhaps you should accept the injustice and trust God to judge. There may be exceptions, but they should remain exactly that: exceptions. The norm should be loving, personal confrontation and forgiveness (Matt 18:15–35; Gal 6:1–2).

SWAPPING METAPHORS: CONQUERING DIVISION IN THE FAMILY

Very few people desire to live in a state of constant conflict. Relational tension, especially in close relationships, is more exhausting than a long run on a hot day. Yet, as long as sin exists, we will have to navigate interpersonal war zones. How, then, do we begin addressing church conflict in healthier, more biblically sound ways? We must first confront Christian consumerism.

Conquering Consumerism

Think about your connection to your local church. Why did you choose your particular church? Did relationships drive your decision, or did you shop around for preaching, music, or a specific ministry that seemed best

18. I know she didn't make up this aphorism, but I'll credit her anyway.

for you? Do your attitudes about serving in your church reveal that your comfort and satisfaction take top priority? Do you attend to worship God and minister to your spiritual family? Or do you walk through the church doors each week singularly focused on "getting something" out of your time? None of us answers these questions perfectly, but we need to admit when consumeristic thinking drives us.

Church samplers also need to re-evaluate their commitment level. When we treat ministries at different churches like a spiritual buffet, we miss the opportunity to know and be known. In effect, our actions reveal that the church exists only to satisfy our spiritual appetites. So, each of us must find one imperfect church to join. Let's devote ourselves to the people, not the activities, ministries, programs, and coffee selection.

If you have the opposite concern and don't want to attend any church of sinners and hypocrites, I encourage you to reconsider. I agree that churches overflow with imperfect people and, in some cases, grade-A jerks. Morally speaking, we all come to Christ from a different starting place, so some believers need to grow a lot before reaching the moral consistency of a new believer who grew up in a strong Christian home.[19] I don't expect my four-year-old to understand why pride is wrong, but I hope he will as an adult. We need to show the same patience with Christians who aren't yet in the same place in the journey of sanctification.

Let's also admit that we're all hypocrites. We have failed to obey Jesus's command to be perfect as God is perfect (Matt 5:48), yet we know and teach this command. Isn't failing to live what you teach the definition of hypocrisy? My point is that the church includes people who struggle with their sinful flesh, and we will continue to struggle until death or Jesus's return. But our weakness only confirms the need for a loving family of fellow disciples to support one another in the hills and valleys.

I beg you, then, to join a church family, anticipating that some people will offend you and others will struggle with hypocrisy. I also challenge you to think back to Christian relationships or churches from which you withdrew in the past. Do you need to reconcile with anyone? Do you need to admit to the pastor or a church member why you left in the first place? Have you stitched together old wounds with the infection of bitterness still inside? If so, take your sibling to coffee and speak the truth in love for your sake and the church's (Gal 5:15–16).

19. This is not to say that a moral unbeliever is better in the eyes of God than an immoral one. Moral or not, Jesus is the only source of eternal life, not our morality. But later in 1 Cor 6, Paul teaches the Corinthians not to sleep with prostitutes, a command many of us had conquered before we confessed faith in Jesus. So, we each start somewhere different on the morality spectrum.

Ministry leaders, you aren't immune from consumerism, so I challenge you to evaluate your ministry stressors. Do you lie awake at night worried about broken marriages and believers flirting with destructive sinful habits? If so, welcome to pastoral ministry. But there's a problem if your focus is the mere perception of success or the apparent satisfaction of certain important people in your congregation. If, like me, you struggle with the people-pleasing disease, then confront the sources of your anxiety. Talk to a trusted friend or counselor about the weight on your shoulders to satisfy others. And determine what success looks like for you in a given task. For example, when it came to Easter and Christmas services, I finally realized (or remembered) that success meant leading our church to exalt God, not to walk away exalting an experience or event. Yes, living out that truth is easier said than done. But we must re-evaluate our priorities as a starting point.

Conquering Conflict

A church that views itself as a family rather than a business will strive to address conflict with healthier, biblical solutions. But conflict won't disappear. Last February, our region saw temperatures drop well below freezing for an extended period. Living in southern Missouri, deep freezes don't come often, so many unprepared homes and buildings in the area suffered damage. Our church building flooded after temperatures returned to normal because our water mains, which run through a poorly insulated ceiling, froze and burst in five places. The water ruined the flooring throughout our building. In the wake of the flood came more decisions than I can count. What kind of replacement flooring should we use in each area? What color is best? Should we add construction? Where do we meet while the installers redo the sanctuary floor? On and on it went.

Along the way, we worked to keep the congregation informed, asked them to vote where appropriate, discussed big decisions as a pastoral team, and left endless details to our vocational pastors. Inevitably, though, someone didn't like the new carpet we chose, not because that person hated the church or lived deeply entrenched in unconfessed sin. Some people just don't like grey. So, when conflict arises, no matter the issue, how should a family of believers handle it? How will we prevent sin from gaining ground during various disagreements?

With Paul, we begin by confessing that we do not battle flesh and blood but the forces of sin (Eph 6:12). If sin causes conflict, then our solution must include fighting against sin. At this point, you might hope for a detailed game plan for defeating sin, but the New Testament epistles do not give us a new law with rules for every conceivable situation. Rather, Paul typically appeals to the Spirit. "But I say, walk by the Spirit, and you will not carry out the desire of the flesh" (Gal 5:16 NASB). Spirit-filled people inevitably produce spiritual fruit: "love, joy, peace, patience, kindness, goodness, faithfulness, gentleness, self-control" (Gal 5:22–23 NASB). Notice that most of the items in Paul's list affect how we interact with others. You can't be kind or gentle alone. We practice our spiritual fruit together.

Paul issues another broad command that can douse the fire of conflict in a church. In Ephesians 5:21 (author's translation), he writes, "Submit to each another in reverence before Christ." Mutual submission means deferring to one another at all times. My wife does not enjoy eating at Fazoli's, but she goes with me occasionally because she knows I like it. My leg muscles don't like mountain biking, but I participate with my wife because I love her. A church full of people who practice Ephesians 5:21 will not argue, attack, and split—at least not as often. Mutual submission empowered by the Spirit arms us for battle against the power of sin. So as we pray corporately for medical appointments and ask God to bring big crowds to our events, may we add desperate prayers for the Spirit of mutual submission to infiltrate our churches.

Despite our best efforts, believers will sin against one another. At that point, we must look to another powerful weapon: gospel-rooted forgiveness. We forgive as God has forgiven us. For that reason, we must constantly reflect upon the gospel, not putting it on the shelf after getting saved like a recently finished novel. We must consciously shape every thought and decision in light of the life, death, and resurrection of Jesus and the forgiveness available to sinners by grace through faith. So when I struggle to forgive a sibling, I know I need a gospel refresher. God has forgiven me of infinitely more wrongs than any brother or sister has committed against me, so I can forgive. Sometimes, we should tell the person who sinned against us that we have forgiven him. When he knows he hurt us, we should forgive him verbally, face to face. Other times, though, we would do well to follow Paul's implicit advice in 1 Corinthians 6 and overlook the wrong.[20] The sarcastic offhanded comments we endure might fall into the overlook category. Whatever the case, forgiveness is the church's gospel-inspired glue.

20. Paul is not talking about sexual assault or violent fights. We can look to 1 Cor 5 and see that Paul demands the removal of church members involved in habitual sexual sin. But in cases dealing with money, property, or other minor offenses, we can accept the wrong done to us without confrontation.

Conquering the Court of Public Opinion

Sometimes, Spirit-empowered mutual submission fails, and we struggle to forgive. At that point, how do we avoid falling into sin? First, we must resist the temptation to form an angry mob on social media or conduct digital warfare against fellow believers (and Christian organizations). Obedience to Scripture's commands about unity should also prevent us from attacking groups with which fellow church members might identify, including political groups. I know even saying the *p*-word (*politics*) will cause some to tune me out, but when you shoot verbal missiles into a faceless crowd, you're bound to hit a brother or sister. Not all Christians think and vote the same, so our biblical mandate demands that we not sacrifice siblings on the altar of politics. What if your vehement tweets silently destroy your relationship with another Christian? Isn't that relationship valuable enough to cause you to stop? It is if the other person is a sibling.

The same principle applies to gossiping in order to sway church opinion on a person or contentious issue. Even if you are in the right, the end doesn't justify the means. Those of us who are pastors need to confront members who habitually attack other believers. We shouldn't have to patrol our church hallways or surveil Facebook like the kindness police, but God has called us to protect the sheep (Acts 20:28–31). Even if we aren't putting "check for online trolls" on our calendars each week, we can at least point out the sins we do see while on social media. If we wouldn't accept someone berating a fellow believer right in front of us, then we shouldn't accept it in a back hallway or on Twitter. Paul gave us a better way of resolving conflict.

When conflict arises that requires input from others, we would do well to implement wisdom councils. Joseph Hellerman describes local church wisdom councils this way: "No formal structure is employed. The group simply shares a meal together and openly discusses all the pros and cons associated with each option, so that an informed decision can be made with the kind of wisdom that can only come from community input. And then they pray together."[21] I admit I have not seen wisdom councils in person. Still, I think they could revolutionize the way believers evaluate everything from interpersonal conflict to critical life decisions, like where to live or who to marry. What if you formed a council of sages within your church (or multiple councils for larger churches), those people whose age and wisdom carry authority in your congregation? What if single mothers knew where to turn when wrestling with how to parent a wayward child? What if college students could discuss potential career options with a trusted group of

---

21. Hellerman, *When Church Was Family*, 175.

believers? What if a wise council of siblings could mediate the longstanding battle between two families in the church? We could kill the cancerous court of public opinion by trusting the family to lead us with the love and concern that only siblings united by Christ can display.

All of the changes I have suggested require a cultural shift in our churches, not the mere implementation of a few new programs. And cultures don't change overnight. Redefining long-established norms requires ongoing communication from church leaders and a commitment to redefine church life according to biblical standards.

In the next chapter, we turn to the role of pastor. If you are not a pastor, I still encourage you to read the next chapter because, by doing so, you will equip yourself to affirm your pastor in ways that bolster his success. The chapter may also offer insight into the unique temptations of pastoral ministry.

7

A Parent, Not a CEO

The Leadership of the Church

As the president of the corporation and chairman of the board, I, as senior minister, am an ex-officio member of all committees and appoint the chairmen of all these committees to the church board for their approval. By appointing the committee chairmen, by being an ex-officio member of each committee, by being the chief of staff presiding over regular staff meetings, I am able to maintain leadership control over the entire operation of the church, working through the church board, committees and staff. It is our sincere belief that this is the only way to organize a church for successful leadership.

—ROBERT SCHULLER

I'M A CHURCH WAR veteran, and you probably are, too. The barrage lasted a solid six months, but it felt like a decade. I will spare you the gruesome details and refrain from casting myself as the innocent but faithful hero. I wasn't, and my reaction to the war proved my fallibility.

People whom I had loved and ministered to—whom I had visited in the hospital and prayed with in cemeteries—hurt me deeply. And the only way to prevent people from causing me more pain was to retreat into my office, set up my desk as a fortress, and start "pastoring" from a distance. I didn't have time for people anyway because I had ministries to run. I could have a greater impact, I thought, if I focussed on organization and planning and documents. These are the things that make for thriving churches, right? During the following year, I silently laid down the mantle of associate pastor and put on the chief operating officer suit and tie. I was no longer accessible, no longer loving, no longer involved, and no longer really pastoring.

My heart of stone began to soften when a group of singles approached me about starting a young adult ministry. They were honest about their struggles and victories, which allowed me to open up about my many imperfections. We began to love each other actively through prayer and by checking in regularly to see how life was going. We studied Scripture together, wrestling through difficult passages and uncomfortable doctrines. I actually started to like ministry again, I think because I was acting like a pastor again. Our group has grown and changed and added and subtracted over the years, but I can honestly say they are one of the main reasons I love the church today.

My ministry joy is no longer planning, speaking, singing, or pulling off a successful event. Big crowds don't satisfy me, and personal compliments have lost their luster. What fills me up is a small group of dedicated people who love me, faults and all. In a church of several hundred, our small group provided something I was missing in our larger gatherings: relationships. But ministry publishing trends show that we don't want to read about how much some guy loves his church family. We want the secrets to success.

IF THE CHURCH IS A BUSINESS, PASTORS RUN THE COMPANY

"The key to successful pastoral ministry is leadership." That's the implicit subtitle of a majority of ministry conferences and popular books for pastors. For example, consider the top twelve leadership books according to a trendy ministry website:[1]

- The Bible

- *Good to Great: Why Some Companies Make the Leap . . . and Others Don't* by Jim Collins

- *The Twenty-One Irrefutable Laws of Leadership: Follow Them and People Will Follow You* by John Maxwell

---

1. Hilgemann, "Best Leadership Books for Pastors."

- *The Seven Habits of Highly Effective People: Powerful Lessons in Personal Change* by Stephen R. Covey

- *Courageous Leadership* by Bill Hybels

- *Leadership Axioms: Powerful Leadership Proverbs* by Bill Hybels

- *Seven Habits of Effective Ministry* by Andy Stanley

- *Next Generation Leader: Five Essentials for Those Who Will Shape the Future* by Andy Stanley

- *EntreLeadership: Twenty Years of Practical Business Wisdom from the Trenches* by Dave Ramsey

- *The Five Dysfunctions of a Team: A Leadership Fable* by Patrick Lencioni

- *Spiritual Leadership: A Commitment to Excellence for Every Believer* by J. Oswald Sanders

- *The Catalyst Leader: Eight Essentials for Becoming a Change Maker* by Brad Lomenick

I'm thankful the Bible appears first on the list (though I will argue the Bible subverts if not outright contradicts the other eleven entries). The second book, *Good to Great*, doesn't claim to be religious in any way. The third, while written by a believer, does not espouse a Christian perspective or biblical foundation. Stephen Covey, who wrote the next book, practiced Mormonism throughout his life, though his book is non-religious. Then we get to books by megachurch pastors (Hybels and Stanley), one of whom eventually resigned under duress; a non-practicing Catholic (Lencioni, who became a practicing Catholic after publishing); and Christian leadership and finance gurus (Ramsey, Sanders, and Lomenick).

Such books are standard texts in many seminary courses designed for pastors. These books also drastically outsell every popular theology or Bible study book by hundreds of thousands of copies. Yet, beyond the Bible, only one of the top leadership books pastors should read explicitly begins with a "spiritual"—if not strictly biblical—perspective.

I intend to demonize none of these authors, though I lament the assumption that these books will make someone a better pastor. How have these leadership manifestos become the standard fare of modern ministers? The obsession with secular leadership principles is a natural outcome of the corporate-church model that treats the pastor as a CEO. But is a pastor really a ministry executive? What exactly *is* a pastor?

The Beginnings of the CEO Pastor

One early church growth writer, Robert Schuller, baldly depicts the pastor as a full-time employee who organizes for a living. "Leadership then rests in the hands of full-time salaried people. If I were a capitalist financing an enterprise, I would insist that the unchallenged leadership be placed in the hands of full-time thinkers and planners. As a pastor heading up a church, I insist on the same."[2] Notice that Schuller's logic for what a pastor *is* depends on a comparison to the business world. The business world comparisons don't stop there, since the very titles Schuller uses for his role betray his sense of what a pastor *is*. Look back at the titles included in the quotation at the beginning of this chapter. Schuller writes, "As the *president* of the corporation and *chairman of the board* . . . the *chief of staff* . . . I am able to maintain leadership control."[3] For Schuller, leadership means that one man controls the church as president, chairman, and chief of staff. He holds all the cards, appointing his subordinates and running their meetings. He is the visionary and the chief executive who will ensure that the church carries out his ideas to produce the greatest results.

If church attendance is any indication, Schuller was right. He was one of the earliest megachurch pastors with enviable attendance numbers and a massive budget. He built a mainly glass three-thousand-seat auditorium dubbed the Crystal Cathedral in 1980 for the modern equivalent of fifty million dollars. In many ways, Schuller was the ultimate CEO pastor, a beckoning model of success. But when he retired, everything fell apart.

Schuller's building projects left the church under crushing debt, and his children fought for control over the empire. In the end, the church ousted the Schuller family, declared bankruptcy, disbanded, and left the Schullers with little to show for their half-century of ministry.[4] Schuller's son has now written a book about personal loss.[5]

Weeping Willow

Schuller began writing on church growth and pastoral leadership over forty years ago, but his legacy lives on. Consider the recent job posting for the senior pastor position at Willow Creek (following the removal of founding

2. Robert H. Schuller, *Your Church Has Real Possibilities*, 52–53.
3. Robert H. Schuller, *Your Church Has Real Possibilities*, 55 (emphasis added).
4. Lavietes, "Rev. Robert Schuller."
5. Robert A. Schuller, *When You Are Down.*

pastor Bill Hybels).[6] The job description begins, "The role: Leading from the South Barrington campus, the Senior Pastor will wear the dual hats of pastor (able to discern God's direction for the congregation) as well as CEO (with organizational leadership skills to lead a complex organization with more than 350 employees). This leader will bring the right balance of preserving what is, but also will fan the flames of Willow's DNA of boldness, innovation, and creativity."

If you read too quickly, you may have missed that this job is for a pastor. The only biblical words that appear are *pastor* and the phrase "God's direction for the congregation." Otherwise, you might confuse this with a job description for the CEO of Berkshire Hathaway or Apple. Willow Creek clearly desires a CEO pastor with a divine vision and the habits of a highly effective person. Sadly, the pastor's primary role is not to shepherd people, disciple believers, or proclaim the truth of the gospel but to "fan the flames of Willow's DNA of boldness, innovation, and creativity"—to build the brand.

Admittedly, the full job description contains bright spots like the qualification that candidates have "an authentic walk with Jesus," but the overall tenor leaves me queasy. Scot McKnight, a one-time Willow member, agrees, warning that several terms are missing from the job description. He writes, "First, no Jesus, no Christ, no Bible, no gospel—that is, in the main words. They are buried into tiny words or they are not there. Amazing. Jesus appears twice. Christ once. God four times. Bible not at all. Gospel not at all. What's a pastor job description without these terms prominent?"[7] Keep in mind that Willow Creek oozes success in every quantifiable way. They're a big church with lots of money and vast influence.

I do not doubt that God has used Willow Creek to save many souls. The church has hosted popular ministry and leadership conferences over the years, too. And their numeric success demands they find someone to manage their vast resources rather than a person to pastor individual lives. I respect that they need an administrator, but I wish they would drop the title *pastor* and stick with *CEO* alone. I appreciate that large churches need administrators to steward the resources God has given. In many ways, this is what the proto-deacons in Acts 6 did for the apostles. But Willow Creek's expectations confuse two distinct roles. Many pastors and churches look to Willow Creek as an example of what pastoral ministry should be, and the dual-hat CEO-pastor position muddies the waters.

6. Vanderbloemen, https://www.vanderbloemen.com/job/willow-creek-community-church-senior-pastor, accessed September 16, 2019.

7. McKnight, "Willow Creek, What's a Pastor?" https://www.patheos.com/blogs/jesuscreed/2019/09/16/willow-creek-whats-a-pastor/.

The Anatomy of a CEO Pastor

Recent statistics show that these trends aren't unique to Willow Creek. Pastors don't like the personal, pastoral part of the job. They like to preach and lead but want to avoid the messes of their congregants' lives. The Barna Group recently asked pastors to pick one aspect of ministry they like the most. Preaching, developing leaders, and organizing comprised 78 percent of the tally. Only 8 percent chose "discipling believers" and 5 percent picked "pastoral care."[8] Another poll asked pastors how they spend their time. Ed Stetzer summarizes, "Many pastors, however, find it difficult to make time for two primary ways of relating to church members and prospects: counseling and visitation. While 24 percent say they spend six hours a week or more in counseling ministry, the same percentage reports spending an hour or less. . . . Forty-eight percent say they spend between two and five hours a week in visitation."[9]

Statistics never tell the whole story, but I'm not surprised that pastors like to (and, thus, choose to) spend their ministry hours locked away in an office or surrounded by a small group of other leaders. And they shy away from hospital visits, counseling congregation members struggling to live out their faith, or sitting with elderly saints who might otherwise feel the church doesn't value them. Why bother holding up brothers and sisters sinking under the weight of a broken world if doing so isn't really what a pastor does? If he's a CEO, that is.

Compare the CEO of Amazon, who leads a workforce the size of a small country (Estonia's population is close, at 1.3 million people).[10] With so many employees, no one expects the CEO to sit with a warehouse manager's family while the manager undergoes surgery. I imagine few people ever look into the eyes of the company's top leaders. Amazon employees expect the executive suite to set the vision and keep the company afloat. Similarly, the articulate and organized CEO pastor doesn't need to care about people as long as the church's attendance and budget grow. Again, I respect that ministry looks different depending on church size, but I also question whether we can faithfully pastor from a distance. Does the CEO pastor really pastor?

If a pastor is a CEO, what qualities should we expect him to embody? According to the *Harvard Business Review*'s ten-year study called the CEO Genome Project, four behaviors determine the success of a CEO:[11]

8. Infographics in Leaders and Pastors, "Ups and Downs of Ministry."
9. Stetzer, "How Protestant Pastors Spend."
10. Soper, "Amazon Now Employs."
11. Botelho et al., "What Sets Successful CEOs Apart."

- Making quick decisions
- Satisfying stakeholders
- Implementing proactive changes
- Reliably producing results

Such attributes equip business leaders to compete in the fluctuating world of the modern marketplace. CEOs with these qualities grow large companies and field the inevitable challenges that come their way, all while protecting jobs and the economies of nations.

Before I continue, let me be clear. If you are a business leader reading this book (I'm shocked, but thanks for humoring me!), strive to develop these four qualities. They aren't sinful or misguided, even for believers called to work in the corporate world. When I took on an administrative role at Southwest Baptist University, I ingested all of the corporate leadership material I could find. I needed to learn how to operate not like a pastor but as a manager who sustains and improves an academic department.

My focus in this book, however, is the church. So we must ask whether or not *Harvard Business Review*'s ideal CEO attributes also describe the biblical pastor. Does Scripture align with the wisdom of corporate leadership? To answer these questions, let's consider the potential risks of adopting the four behaviors of a successful CEO.

First, a CEO pastor might spend less time praying and waiting on the Lord because speedy decision-making is ideal. Who has time to pray when decisions must come quickly? Second, the CEO pastor could easily become what Paul referred to as a "man-pleaser," giving preference to those who invest the most money into the church budget (i.e., stakeholders). We once had a pastor from another state advise us to launch a giving campaign by holding an elegant retreat for our biggest tithers. (We didn't.) Third, the successful CEO pastor may dizzy the church with changes to stay ahead of the game. While proactivity is admirable, the visionary can quickly lose sight of the sheep who need shepherding now. Fourth, we have already critiqued the model of ministry that emphasizes measurable results because it easily neglects the truth that only God grows a church.

Maybe I'm overly pessimistic about the risks. The congregation may survive a pastor with such qualities, and God may bring real growth. But are these the attributes we should exalt in a potential minister? My concern is that the church that wants a CEO pastor may not care if he has the attributes Scripture prioritizes for men who aspire to such a role. And to these, we now turn.

IF THE CHURCH IS A FAMILY, THE PASTOR THINKS LIKE A PARENT

We could accept the CEO pastor model if the Bible were silent on pastoral ministry. If we had no examples of gospel ministry in Acts, no reflections on the joys and pains of church planting in 1–2 Corinthians, no warning for shepherds in 1 Peter 5, and no list of qualifications in the Pastoral Epistles, I would gladly line my shelves with the myriad of leadership books available. But, we can learn a lot about pastoring from the New Testament. The New Testament may not exhaust the topic, but it establishes the border a biblical pastor should paint within.

The go-to text for pastoral qualifications is 1 Timothy 3:1–7. Before we jump in, we must remember that Paul didn't write chapters per se, so chapter 3 connects closely to chapter 2. There, Paul gave instructions about who can "teach and hold authority" in the church (2:12), which leads seamlessly into his instructions for "overseers" in chapter 3. The context helps us identify what Paul means by "overseer" in 3:1.

Without getting too technical, the word *overseer* (*episkopos*) is closer to a guardian than a manager. Paul closes the letter with a call for his young pastoral protégé, Timothy, to guard against false teaching. "O Timothy, guard what has been entrusted to you, avoiding worldly and empty chatter and the opposing arguments of what is falsely called 'knowledge'—which some have professed and thus gone astray from the faith. Grace be with you" (1 Tim 6:20–21 NASB). If we follow the instruction Paul gave, we will seek overseers who protect the church, not by organizing ministry programs or leading the leaders but by keeping an eye out for potentially harmful doctrine and behavior. Shepherds guard the sheep.

The first house Emily and I bought was a block away from Doling Park, where we often walked our two dogs. To get to Doling, we had to cross in front of a house with the world's largest Rottweiler. As was typical in our struggling neighborhood, the owners used a rope to tie the dog to a small bush in the front yard. I have trust issues anyway, but the flimsy rope and weak shrubbery did not inspire confidence. Honestly, I would have felt nervous with that dog trapped in Fort Knox. So when the Rottweiler's deafening, phlegm-filled bark echoed through the neighborhood as he jumped and pulled against the rope and bush, I never took my eyes off of him. I didn't have a great plan. I'm pretty sure any weapon I owned would have only made the monster angrier. A wiser man would've carried a pack of beef jerky as a peace offering. But, I watched him with the intent of sacrificing myself if he got free, so my wife could run to safety. I don't claim bravery, but love makes you willing to sacrifice a lot. I think the same is true for Paul's vision of the church guardian—a person we in the evangelical world call *pastor*. He watches the wolves closely to keep the church from falling prey, and he will endure the wolf's bite if necessary for the benefit of his beloved sheep.

The Biblical Pastor's Résumé

A pastor needs to meet specific qualifications to guard the church. Paul begins in 1 Timothy 3:2 with an overarching idea: the pastor must be above reproach. He should live a lifestyle that gives no basis for criticism. Paul doesn't want pastors to obsess over their image, but if a pastor intends to guard the church against false teaching, he must have a good reputation. It's the same reason defense attorneys use character witnesses—to show that when the defendant gives his side of the story, the jury can trust him. For the pastor who may need to claim "He's wrong, and I'm right," character is critical.

Paul goes on to clarify what irreproachable character looks like in practice. In a moment, we will focus on the familial qualification Paul uses in verses 4–5. But let's begin with a brief rundown of the rest of the list in verses 2–3, 6–7 (using the NASB's language), where Paul fleshes out what it means to be above reproach. *The husband of one wife.* Scholars have interpreted this controversial phrase to mean various things: that a pastor cannot be divorced, must be married, must not have multiple wives, needs to remain sexually faithful to his spouse, or about a dozen other points of emphasis. Without bogging ourselves down, we can at least conclude that a sexually promiscuous pastor would fail the test. *Temperate.* A pastor prone to extremes will wreck a church. *Prudent.* This term speaks to self-control and modesty, like the pastor who refuses to exaggerate to make himself look better. *Respectable.* If you are a contrarian who always wants to push boundaries and doesn't care if you rub people the wrong way, you're out. *Hospitable.* A pastor makes people feel like treasured guests, not interruptions. *Able to teach.* A necessity for fighting against falsehood. *Not addicted to wine.* (Goes without saying.) *Not pugnacious.* I wish he meant "doesn't like pugs," but Paul means a pastor shouldn't bully people. *Gentle.* He tolerates people who rub him the wrong way. *Peaceable.* A pastor should not start fights. *Free from the love of money.* Paul recognizes how easy it would be to abuse the pastoral position, and he returns to the issue of money in 6:17–19. *Not a new convert.* The reason is not that the neophyte is untrained but that he might think he is better than everyone else—imitating the devil's pride. *A good reputation with those outside the church.* Paul wants to prevent a pastor from becoming a firebrand on Twitter.

The Fatherly Qualifications

Alone, these thirteen qualifications stand as a concrete median between those heading down the highway of CEO-style pastoral leadership and those driving toward a biblical image of the pastorate. The CEO's qualifications relate to efficiency and acumen, while the biblical pastor's focus on character. But, we still haven't touched on a crucial familial qualification to which Paul devotes the most ink of any item in his list.

What is the ultimate predictor of pastoral success? Not advanced academic degrees. Not success in growing a business. Instead, *he manages his own household well.* Some translate the term *manage* as *lead,* though Paul uses a parallel verb in verse 5 that means "to care for." Paul does not depict a distant CEO running the affairs of a vast estate.[12] Instead, he pictures a father who lovingly guides his children into truth, who teaches them to respect authority, who models dignified behavior for them (v. 4). Recall that Paul is not a father, at least not in the traditional sense. Yet, he affectionately speaks of his children often. Paul's churches are his kids, whom he rebukes and labors over as a parent (1 Cor 4:14; 2 Cor 12:14; Gal 4:19). Timothy is Paul's "beloved and faithful child in the Lord" (1 Cor 4:17; see also Phil 2:22; 1 Tim 1:2, 18; 2 Tim 1:2; 2:1), as are Titus (Titus 1:4) and Onesimus (Phlm 10). If Paul parents affectionately, we can assume that he also expects a candidate for overseer to love, protect, rebuke, and encourage his children—his church. So, how a man treats his physical children is a good indicator of what kind of minister he will be.

Most translations place verse 5 in parentheses, but Paul's explanation isn't a meaningless aside. Paul asks, "But if a man does not know how to manage his own household, how will he take care of the church of God?" We could reword Paul's question as a negative statement: if a man does not know how to lead his family, *he will not care for the family of God well.* The logic of connecting family life and church life becomes clear later in the chapter. Paul explains, "I write so that you will know how one ought to conduct himself in the *household* of God, which is the church of the living God, the pillar and support of the truth"[13] (1 Tim 3:15b NASB, emphasis added). Paul defines the qualifications for pastors and deacons in order to prepare

12. Admittedly, a wealthy father in the ancient world might function this way, but two factors prevent us from importing it into Paul. First, the emphasis in our passage is how the father treats his kids. Second, it is unlikely that Paul's audience consisted primarily of the uber-wealthy. Probably, the mixed congregation could identify better with a small, affectionate, lower-class family.

13. For a defense of the view that 3:14–15 represents the purpose statement of 1 Timothy and that stewarding the Christian household is the controlling idea, see Tomlinson, "Purpose and Stewardship Theme."

Timothy and others to protect the local family of God—the household that stands for truth. So, we shouldn't wonder why Paul spends so much time on the fatherly qualification for pastors (and then mentions it again as a qualification for deacons). The church is a family, and the pastor must act like a good parent.

Mother Paul

Paul didn't apply parenting language only to would-be pastors. He thought of himself as a complete parenting unit—father and mother. That Paul considered himself a spiritual father isn't surprising, since he was a man and thought of his churches and co-workers as his children. What shocks us is that Paul could picture himself as a mother. In Gal 4:19 (CSB), Paul painfully admits, "My children, I am again suffering labor pains for you until Christ is formed in you." Paul did not consider the pain of fatherhood a sufficient illustration of his deep concern for the Galatians. Since Paul refers to suffering labor pains "again," we can presume that his initial work of church planting figuratively birthed the churches of Galatia into existence. And yet, as mothers soon recognize, childbirth is only the beginning of a mom's suffering.

I know my wife's heart broke when my five-year-old daughter came home from kindergarten and reported that a classmate excluded and insulted her. (I just got angry, by the way, and fought the urge to show up at recess the next day and knock that bully off the monkey bars. But, I asked Rylie what she should do, and she said she wanted to pray for the child! I felt three millimeters tall.) Paul knew what it was like to see his babies fail to reach their potential, to languish in immaturity. And as a good pastoral parent, it hurt him deeply.

Another passage where Paul plays the mother card is 1 Thessalonians 2:7. Leading up to the passage, Paul condemns a ministry style that prioritizes people-pleasing (v. 4), flattering an audience (v. 5), greed (v. 5), seeking recognition (v. 6), and an authoritarian style of leadership (v. 6). Paul's ministry was different. "But we proved to be gentle among you, as a nursing mother tenderly cares for her own children. Having so fond an affection for you, we were well-pleased to impart to you not only the gospel of God but also our own lives, because you had become very dear to us" (1 Thess 2:7–8 NASB). Here, Paul's motherly ministry is not one of pain but of comfort and affection. As a minister, Paul was willing to die for his children, the Thessalonian Christians. I imagine few CEOs would say the same about their employees. But moms understand Paul's sentiment immediately.

The Parental Pastor Paradigm

Altogether, these passages sketch an image of a parental pastor with seven essential qualities. The first two broad qualities do not necessarily reflect a parental view of the pastorate, but the other five do.

1. First, at his core, the parental pastor is a *guardian*. He watches for signs of danger, particularly theological threats, though 1 Timothy mentions dissension just as often. When the tumor of unorthodoxy creeps in, he administers the anesthetic of fatherly care and starts cutting away the error. I believe many modern pastors take this role seriously, but they see it playing out mostly through their preaching ministries. I think the biblical guardian is more personal than that. He talks, but he also listens. He preaches, but he also engages believers in conversation. In short, he cannot fulfill the role of guardian standing behind a pulpit. Instead, he guards by watching the children closely and knowing them personally. Only the pastor who knows and is known can protect his church.

2. According to Paul, the second defining qualification of a pastor is that he is *blameless*. So, while this quality isn't strictly parental, it is biblical and must become part of the paradigm. *Blameless* does not mean perfect. But, it does mean that a candidate with a noticeable moral flaw or a reputation for sinfulness should not become a pastor. How can he guide and guard a congregation if they can't trust his character? Now on to five qualities unique to the parental pastor model.

3. He is a loving *guide*. He doesn't only guard against poor theology, but he leads the congregation to Scripture. Since the pastor must know what is biblical if he is to guide the family, saturation in Scripture is key. This is why I believe in theological education. Many pastors minister effectively without earning an academic degree, but I think they could serve even better with theological education. At the very least, I know they would come to love Scripture more deeply through the influence of wise, godly professors.

4. The parental pastor *models* faith. Modeling requires personal presence. He cannot demonstrate how to live a God-honoring life from afar, not even through a preaching ministry. People must see the highs and lows of the parental pastor. The church should watch him suffer well and succeed humbly. And unlike the CEO pastor, the parental pastor's job isn't merely task-oriented. Modeling a godly life isn't about

getting something done but about being a certain kind of person. And, by the way, the results of this quality aren't easily measurable.

5. He affectionately *encourages and rebukes*. When my daughter was five years old, I taught her how to ride a bike without training wheels. At one point, I ran down the sidewalk with my hands around her waist as she tried to balance her bicycle. At another point, I rode her pink Minnie Mouse bike to show her it *is* possible. As a dad, I had a balancing act to do: firmly forcing her to do something scary while warmly encouraging her when she struggled. This is the vision of the parental pastor. He isn't merely dictating changes from a boardroom table. He's in the trenches, holding hands with his church family as they pursue Christ together. He may need to reprimand them at times, but the church never doubts his love. He only challenges them for their good.

6. He *weeps* when his children do something stupid. Pastoring and conflict go hand in hand. We cannot avoid pettiness and selfishness when we're pastoring human beings. So, how does the parental pastor respond? Unlike the CEO pastor, he doesn't say, "Get on board or get out," with only the company's bottom line in mind. He doesn't run from a challenge, doesn't lead like an authoritarian dictator, and doesn't let anger shape his reactions. No, the parental pastor's heart breaks when sin creeps into the community. His brokenness comes not from fear that their immaturity will reflect poorly on his leadership but from a deep desire to see his family become more like Christ. He rebukes like a brokenhearted mother whose love doesn't change based on how her child acted today. The parental pastor is someone who struggling people want to be around.

7. He *comforts* his suffering children. This is pastoral care. Let me be blunt: the pastor who is too busy with executive board meetings and sermon prep to cry with mourning church family members *is not pastoring*. I'm not saying he has to pastor everyone equally. I would argue that I'm the pastor of my young adult ministry much more than Springhill's senior pastor is (and he agrees). That's how it should work. But a pastor needs to re-evaluate his role if he is not personally invested in the lives of his church family, if he never lies awake in bed trying to pray instead of only worrying about them. Our church family endures cancer, genetic disorders, car crashes, and funerals. And these things can't simply pass pastors by. Every minister must be a God-given means of comfort among our church family.

Pastors who exhibit these seven qualities and who think about ministry through the eyes of a parent are well on their way to living out the biblical image of a pastor. But, how do we get there?

SWAPPING METAPHORS: TURNING MANAGERS INTO MINISTERS

Inevitably, leadership manuals stumble upon biblical wisdom from time to time. A good CEO is humble, selfless, and focused on what matters. These are biblical values. But occasional crossover doesn't redeem the CEO pastor paradigm. If ministers must defend how biblical their leadership models are, they might have the cart before the horse. Why go to another text and try to prove it is biblical when you can simply start with Scripture? More importantly, while some leadership values are good, many others aren't. Remember, a CEO's job is to increase profits. Period. The same is not true of the biblical pastor.

Like parenting, the pastoral role is inherently relational rather than task-driven. Of course, prioritizing relationships does not eliminate the need for good old-fashioned hard work. Parents pay bills, take out the trash, and fix the roof. They spend time cleaning and preparing budgets. They may even set goals for their family to move to a better school district or save money for vacations. But these tasks don't define parenting even when they take up most of the week. Good parents complete tasks for a purpose: to make space for healthy relationships.

Likewise, pastors have tasks to complete, but relationships should remain the priority. Depending on the church's size, a pastor may take the lead on everything from cleaning toilets to securing bank loans. Ministers of all varieties must think about budgets and buildings. These tasks, however, cannot become ends unto themselves. The purpose of pastoral ministry is to shepherd a flock, to lead a family with a love that is equal parts compassion and protection. Tasks aren't the purpose. People are.

Those of us who, if we're honest, enjoy ministry tasks more than connecting with people should strive to build biblical community into our ministries. Therefore, I encourage every minister to find a small, consistent group of believers to treat like family. Let's admit that preaching at people for thirty minutes each week doesn't build the kind of relationships all believers need, especially for ministers who constantly pour out. Preaching is critical, but you also need a small group of siblings you can learn to love. I know it feels awkward as a pastor to invest in some people more than others, like you're playing favorites with your children. But if you feel guilty, remember that Jesus chose twelve out of his multitude of followers and then invested even more relational equity in Peter, James, and John. Tell your congregation that you practice what you preach, and assure them that you are still their pastor. Then, let the small group minister to your soul.

Climbing the Church Ladder

On a related note, I fear for the future of vocational ministry as the career-driven pastor becomes the norm. For example, let's say our imaginary friend, Pastor Josh, applies for a youth pastor position immediately out of college, intending to stay at the church only long enough to pad his résumé so a larger church might consider him. Along the way, he begins developing his platform on social media and through personal contacts at conferences. Three years later, Pastor Josh "moves up" to an associate pastoral role at a church twice the size of his first employer and begins promoting himself on LinkedIn as a dynamic conference speaker. Another three years pass, and Josh is ready to pursue a senior pastor position at a traditional church with moderate attendance numbers. He knows he must produce results, since he will never move up the ministry ladder if the church doesn't increase numerically. Josh has also met some big names in the Christian leadership industry while speaking at conferences, and he begs one best-selling author to allow Josh to co-author the next big ministry book. With a book on the horizon and increasing attendance on Sunday mornings, Josh makes his move after only two years at his current church. He applies for a lead pastor position at a bonafide megachurch. After landing the job, Josh begins publishing books on his own, gains thousands of Twitter followers, and is invited to headline a high-profile ministry conference. He has arrived. And thousands of young college and seminary students training for ministry look to him as a model of true success.

You may read this hypothetical narrative and wonder what the problem could be. Josh was an imitable success story, right? Maybe he simply followed God's lead and was blessed. Perhaps the Spirit opened and shut doors, just as he did with Paul and Silas on the second missionary journey. But the story hints at a few red flags for Josh. First, Josh spent eight years in pastoral ministry at churches he never intended to pastor. He did not stay long enough to know the struggles and joys of the church family and, more importantly, to be known. And while he likely appeared to put the church first, Josh's selfish interests inevitably drove much of his decision-making.

If we replace *church* with *wife* or *family*, the error of Josh's ways becomes clearer. Imagine that Josh marries a moderately attractive woman

from a low-income family in hopes of leaving her in a few years for a beautiful, wealthy woman. If Josh deserted his children every three years and
started a new family in hopes of landing a group of gifted and obedient
children, we would consider him psychotic. But among church families, this
cycle of abandonment has become the norm.

We accept career-driven ministry because moving up and out constantly happens in the business world. We don't fault new lawyers for hoping
to make partner. Even I hope to make full professor someday, once I pay my
dues. But vocational ministry is unlike any career. We see no evidence in the
New Testament that overseers or elders sought to move to larger congregations or gain a position at the mother church in Jerusalem. The only leaders
concerned about their positions are the super-apostles Paul so passionately
opposes in the Corinthian letters.

But when we ignore the tendencies of career-driven pastors, the results
can be devastating. Some orphaned churches have gone decades without
experiencing the love and dedication of a committed parental pastor. Others hire a new pastor more often than Americans vote for a president, generating a sense of distrust. The habitually abandoned congregation typically
refuses to follow someone who will hit the road when the next crisis comes.

The cycle harms pastors, too. Their desire to move up often breeds
discontentment and bitterness toward their current church. They so eagerly
desire the supposed ease and renown that comes from pastoring a large
church, not to mention the salary, that anything less seems like a waste of
time. In the end, the congregation becomes a tool to fix the broken ambition
that drives them.

The Path Forward

So, church member, when your current pastor leaves, and you look to hire
a new one, take the search seriously. Write a job description that reflects
your church's understanding of the biblical role and qualifications of a pastor. Don't settle for a generic posting copied from Indeed.com. Search for
a parental pastor. And when you interview, be sure to ask what he believes
successful pastoral ministry looks like. Ask about his personal goals, hopes,
and dreams. Look at his résumé closely and request specific reasons why he
left previous churches. Did exiting another congregation pain him deeply,
or was he excited for new opportunities? And don't let him cop out with
"The Lord told me to go." Have him clarify the ways and means by which
God led him to leave his previous family. These are questions worth asking.

To be clear, I believe the Lord can call a pastor to exit his church family graciously, but I also know God deeply desires shepherds who are committed to their sheep. We should celebrate pastors who spend decades guiding a single church for richer or poorer, for better or worse, in sickness and in health. We should honor a faithful pastor as we would a devoted parent. And we, as people under God-given authority, should follow their lead. (By the way, please don't use this chapter to beat up your ministry staff if they haven't yet bought into the parental pastor model. Engage in loving conversations, and trust the work of the Spirit.)

Pastors, I strongly encourage you to evaluate your view of ministry. How do you define success? Who are exemplary ministers you admire? A constant theme of this book has been that the resources we ingest will shape our actions. What, then, are you reading? To what podcasts do you listen? What ministry leaders do you follow on social media? And what do those resources reveal about your view of ministry success? Evaluate these resources for their conformity to Scripture, and beware of those that ignore biblical imagery to promote the corporate-church model.[14] Don't let them redefine what God designed the church and pastor to be.

If you're in vocational ministry, what do you love about your job? Do you love ministering to people? Or do you love the business of the church? If you're most passionate about administration, could it be that God designed you to serve him as a Fortune 500 CEO or a corporate administrator? If you love Jesus but dread spending time with hurting people, maybe God has a calling for you outside of pastoral ministry. And that's okay.

I often see this confusion in first-year college students. They love Christ and recognize that God has given them unique skills, so vocational ministry seems like the natural route. But maybe God wants to use them in the business world, evangelizing a group of people only an entrepreneur can reach and ministering in their local churches as faithful volunteers. It isn't sinful to choose a profession other than ministry, but it is sinful to force the church to become a business in order to fill a void in your life. I long for every person God has called to vocational ministry to live out the calling resiliently. But I also pray God will give courage to those who shouldn't be pastors but are afraid to let go. Maybe your church even has room for an administrator position that doesn't claim to be pastoral. Whatever the result, God is sovereign over both your personal needs and the shepherding of his church. Trust him.

14. If you don't have the biblical and theological foundation to critique your resources, let me recommend seeking academic training at a good college or seminary.

Let me close this chapter by suggesting a three-tier evaluation that any minister can perform. The evaluation isn't quantitative because only honest reflection will reveal the results of this test. The three tiers refer to three people who should evaluate your ministry. First, you should evaluate yourself because no one else knows the true motives of your heart. Second, ask a trusted staff member or leader to assess your ministry because that person knows your blind spots. Depending on your church size, it may be best to have a third party select and communicate with the individual to protect the evaluator and encourage honesty. Finally, ask a church member to evaluate you. Again, depending on how you receive criticism, you may need to utilize a third party to act as a mediator, so the church member can remain anonymous. All three tiers should describe how the minister lives out the seven essential qualities of a parental pastor:

- Does the minister guard the church from dissension, false teaching, and sin?
- Does the minister live a blameless life before the church and outsiders?
- Does the minister guide the church toward Scripture with clarity?
- Does the minister model faith by living a godly life?
- Does the minister lovingly encourage and rebuke with discernment?
- Does the minister respond to immaturity with sorrow rather than anger, blame, or apathy?
- Does the minister comfort those who suffer?

No minister is perfect, so the purpose of the three-tier evaluation is to identify areas for the Lord to grow you, not to provide another reason to beat yourself up. The evaluation also focuses everyone's attention on what a minister truly is—not a CEO but a parent.

8

Where Do We Go from Here?

As I WRAP UP writing this book, I am recovering from a broken clavicle. It happened one night when my riding lawn mower was not cutting evenly. I used some spare lumber to build a ramp so I could look underneath the heavy machine. After working for an hour and failing to solve the problem, I gave up. Looking at the ramp I built, I realized it would make an excellent ramp for my mountain bike.

As will become clear, I'm not much of a mountain biker, but my athletic wife had recently taken to it. We've been married twelve years, but I still want to impress her or, at the very least, hold on to my man card. So, I upcycled the mower ramp into a sturdy bike ramp. Emily had taken our kids to get snow cones, leaving me alone at the house. Naturally, I decided to test the new ramp, maybe mastering a few moves to show off when she got home. I hopped on my bike, gained some speed, and hit the ramp. To my credit, the ramp held up. It really was sturdy. Unfortunately, physics is not my forte. As I flew up the ramp at top speed, I thought, "This seems too steep." Once both wheels left the ramp, I realized that the only parts of my body still connected to the bike were my fingertips. I had a split-second decision to make. Land on the bike or bail out. I bailed, rolling to my right side. I floated through the air for several minutes, or so it seemed at the time. But when I landed shoulder first on the ground, reality hit with me. I immediately grabbed my shoulder and felt a noticeable bump where there wasn't one before. My first thought was, "How much is this going to cost?"

By the time I had made it fifty yards to my back door, I was feeling pretty woozy. I practically collapsed just inside the house. By God's grace, I had my phone, so I called my wife right away. I guess I described the injury, saying, "I wrecked my bike, and now a bone is sticking out." Maybe I should have said, "There's a new bump on my shoulder," because my wife entered the house a few minutes later expecting to find a bloody bone shard protruding from my body. When she arrived, I instantly felt safe. I knew she would take care of me because she loves me. I just didn't realize how much I would need her over the next few weeks.

Shoulder pain makes every activity difficult. Putting on a T-shirt is nearly impossible. Drying off after a shower or sneezing can drop you to your knees. The doctor told me not to drive, so I needed a chauffeur. As a righty with a broken right clavicle, I was useless when it came to cooking, washing dishes, mowing the lawn, picking up our kids, and just about every other helpful activity. Not to mention, I grew frustrated with my limitations and needed someone to calm me down and remind me of the bigger picture. Emily steered our family through a rough few weeks with grace. In all of our years together, I have never loved and respected her more than I do today. Her compassionate, do-whatever-it-takes attitude perfectly models how the New Testament envisions believers should relate to one another.

A CALL TO BROTHERLY LOVE

We have spent most of our time in the Pauline epistles, but other New Testament authors thought of the church as a family, too. One of the most family-oriented books in Scripture is the sermon we know as Hebrews. The author of Hebrews uses familial themes in unique ways in comparison to Paul. Hebrews emphasizes that Jesus is the Son of God and presents believers as Christ's siblings. To wrap up, then, we will trace the argument of Hebrews from beginning to end and notice how the author puts together many of the themes we have emphasized throughout this book.

Jesus as Son

Hebrews begins by proving that Jesus is the Son.[1] The author of Hebrews contrasts the messages of prophets and angels with that of the Son, the heir

---

1. See Peeler, *You Are My Son*; Gray, "Brotherly Love."

apparent. Sonship makes Christ the better messenger because he alone fully knows the mind of God. There's no comparison. If you wanted to know me better, you would ask my wife, not my dog. We see the same degree of difference between the way Jesus communicates God and how angels do. Jesus, the Son, can speak the Father's language but is also fluent in humanity. Consequently, Jesus can serve in a unique role as the Great High Priest, the ultimate mediator between God and man.

According to Hebrews, Jesus also ministers as the brother of humanity. What's the family link? According to Heb 2:11 (NASB), "For both He who sanctifies and those who are sanctified are all from one Father; for which reason He is not ashamed to call them brethren." As believers, we share a Father with Jesus, making us Jesus's brothers and sisters. And he is a wonderful older brother. The early believers would have expected the oldest brother to take care of his siblings. Around the time the New Testament was written, the philosopher Plutarch wrote a book about brotherly love. He mentions that outsiders might mock a lesser sibling for failing to live up to his brother's lofty reputation. Plutarch suggests a response the lesser sibling could give, writing, "'Not so,' a sensible man would reply. 'I have a brother who is highly esteemed, and most of his influence is mine to share.'"[2] For the author of Hebrews, Jesus shares his high esteem with his siblings, removing all traces of shame for believers. All the good things Jesus possesses are ours to share.

Jesus also offers practical aid according to Hebrews. He helps his siblings overcome Satan's reign of fear (2:14) and intercedes as a merciful and faithful high priest (2:17a), atoning for the people (2:17b). Since Jesus knows temptation, he helps his weaker siblings who face temptation during times of suffering (2:18). Jesus supports and protects his siblings because that's what older brothers do (at least according to the ancient mindset). The compassion of Jesus didn't end at the cross but continues on today. He is an excellent big brother.

Believers as Siblings

After chapter 2, the author of Hebrews does not saturate his sermon with sibling language. Instead, he signals the familial root metaphor at critical junctures: Heb 3:1, 12; 10:19; 13:1, 22. The author first addresses his audience as brothers in 3:1, immediately following his promise that Jesus helps his tempted siblings (2:18). Hebrews 3:1 (NASB) says, "Therefore, holy brethren, partakers of a heavenly calling, consider Jesus, the Apostle

2. Plutarch, *Frat. amor.*, 16E (Helmbold, LCL).

and High Priest of our confession." Why does the author start this section with sibling language? He does so because believers in distress should look to their older brother for help. Consider the author's subtle warning a few verses later in 3:6 (NASB), "Christ was faithful as a Son over His house— whose house we are, if we hold fast our confidence and the boast of our hope firm until the end." How do we know we're children of God? Like Jesus, we possess an enduring hope. Think of it this way. If Jesus considers those he sanctifies as siblings (2:11), and if he helps his siblings avoid temptation while suffering (2:18), then maintaining hope during sorrow is the ultimate proof that one belongs to the family (3:6). Jesus's brothers and sisters bear the scars and calluses that prove they have survived hardship.

Guitar players prize calluses. When I taught students to play the guitar, two factors divided those who would become players from those whose guitars would become decorations. The first was rhythm. Some have it, and some don't. People think of learning the guitar as memorizing chords, but rhythm is the hard part. Yet, another factor matters even more: endurance. When you start playing the piano or drums, your hands and fingers feel fine. Not so with the guitar. The first few hours of pushing metal strings down with your fingertips cause real pain. Day 2 isn't any better. In fact, thick calluses don't appear for several months. As a teenager, I eventually developed thick calluses that protected me and made my musical journey possible. Biblical endurance works the same way. As we see God sustain us time and again, we build up faith calluses against the pains of everyday life. When suffering comes, the mature believer can endure with hope—not a false hope that ignores the reality of suffering but a steadfast hope built upon years of depending on a faithful older brother.

Our Brothers' Keepers

Sibling language next appears when the author issues a community-focused warning in 3:12–13 (NASB), writing, "Take care, brethren, that there not be in any one of you an evil, unbelieving heart that falls away from the living God. But encourage one another day after day, as long as it is still called 'Today,' so that none of you will be hardened by the deceitfulness of sin." In this case, sibling language recalls not the audience's relationship to their superior brother, Jesus, but the devoted relationship between believers. If believers don't take up arms together, battling every day to prevent sin from gaining ground, disaster might overtake the weak. Keep in mind that Hebrews envisions a community of believers who interact daily. Of course, they couldn't Zoom or text one another, so their daily gatherings usually took place early in the morning. We have the advantage of instant communication, so it shouldn't be hard to encourage one another every day. A text message, phone call, or simple note can make a world of difference. And when the stakes rise, so does our level of encouragement. Here's a good rule of thumb: the greater their temptation, the greater our exhortation.

To answer Cain's question in Genesis 3, we are indeed our brothers' keepers. We desperately need one another to survive the daily battle against sin and doubt. Hand in hand, we continue on the journey together to ensure that none fall along the way as the Israelites did in the wilderness (Heb 3:17–19). For Hebrews, the end of the journey is God's rest, leading the author to warn his audience, writing, "Therefore let us be diligent to enter that rest, so that no one will fall" (Heb 4:11a NASB). We, the church family, encourage and exhort daily so that no individual brother and sister stumbles.

The author does not address the audience as siblings again until 10:19, where he closes the main body of his sermon and draws initial conclusions. "Therefore, brethren, since we have confidence to enter the holy place by the blood of Jesus" (NASB), begins the author, who then gives three exhortations in verses 22–24. Let's draw near to Jesus. Let's cling to our confession. And let's consider how to provoke one another to love and good deeds. Why does the author introduce this pivotal exhortation with sibling language? He does so to recall the paradigm he established in Hebrews 2—the family model. By the way, the author qualifies his command in 10:24–25 to provoke love and good deeds with the instruction "not forsaking our own assembling together, as is the habit of some, but encouraging one another; and all the more as you see the day drawing near" (10:25 NASB). The plea mirrors 3:13, where he called them to gather daily and exhort one another. Families gather, whether digitally or in person, to motivate one another. "I know your day was difficult," we say, "but tomorrow will be better. Hang in there!" Hebrews mixes family language with calls to encourage one another because that's what families do. And without it, we're sunk.

Keep Loving Like Family

The last two references to siblings both occur in the closing chapter of Hebrews. The author begins in 13:1 (CSB), "Let brotherly love continue." I wish our church buildings had this brief verse printed above every door. The pithy command encapsulates the root metaphor underlying the author's exhortations throughout Hebrews. He drew from the well of ancient family life to shape believers' perception of one another, and now he wants them to live like it. For the original audience and us today, living out brotherly love goes beyond Sunday morning handshakes. We act like siblings when we bring meals to families with newborns, when we text a message of prayer before the big interview, when we help our small group leader move across town, when we watch the kids while mom and dad go to counseling, or when we drive for half an hour to the hospital for a visit. Brotherly love isn't an idea but an action.

In Heb 13:22, the final reference to siblings closes Hebrews. "But I urge you, brethren, bear with this word of exhortation, for I have written to you briefly" (NASB). We might argue with the author about the meaning of the word *briefly*, but he clearly hopes his siblings will hear the entire sermon as a brotherly exhortation. I think he meant for Hebrews to become a paradigm for the Christian family to imitate as they exhort one another, alternately warning and encouraging when needed. In the same spirit, Plutarch writes about siblings in the ancient world, "For such a kinsman it is altogether fitting to concede and allow some faults, saying to him when he errs, 'I cannot leave you in your wretchedness and trouble and folly.'"[3] Likewise, the sibling relationship between believers isn't always sugary sweet. The closer our relationships grow, the more faults we notice. Faithful siblings must offer a healthy dose of reality occasionally but should do so with a spoonful of sugary sweetness.[4]

COMMON THREADS

We began this book by arguing that thinking leads to doing. How we think about any area of life—parenting, a career, or the church—will determine our actions. So, if you walk away with no other insight, I hope you will at least evaluate your image of what the church is. In recent years, I have listened closely as everyday Christians talk about their churches. I consistently hear the underlying message that the church is a business. Often, people liken church life to their jobs. Whatever works at work must work at church. I admit that I am tempted to treat Springhill like Southwest Baptist University, my employer. Both seek to honor Christ and teach Scripture faithfully. But one is a school and the other is a family. They aren't the same thing, so they don't do the same thing.

A related thread I have pulled throughout the book is that the materials we regularly ingest shape our understanding of what the church is. Ministry podcasts, blogs, and conferences are great, but we must examine

---

3. Plutarch, *Frat. amor.*, 482A–B (Helmbold, LCL).

4. See the positive comments the author shares about his audience in Heb 6:9–10; 10:32–34, both of which follow harsh warnings.

their underlying root metaphors. If they exalt the corporate-church model, be wary. They influence us more than we like to admit. I know we can "swallow the meat (helpful content) and spit out the bones (unhelpful content)," but two-dollar steaks aren't worth the effort.

Keep in mind that the very book you are now finishing is only as good as it is faithful to Scripture. We have argued throughout that Scripture is not silent on church life and practice, as some assume it to be. After looking at various passages, we must admit that the Bible has a lot to say about the church. No, Paul never gives a formula for determining how many pastors we need based on attendance trends. He doesn't discuss music styles or dictate how often the women's ministry should host events. But Paul and his fellow inspired authors held a clear vision of church life that we must adopt. Scripture tells us what the church is. We must put the gospel-rooted, biblical vision into practice.

For Church Members

Know and be known. I planted statements like this throughout the book because church life involves more than attendance. When I have flown alone out of busy airports, I always experienced the bizarre paradox of feeling alone while surrounded by people. I might sit in the same row as another person and, with that person, obey the instructions of the airline staff. We might eat the same snacks and watch the same movie on the plane. But that doesn't mean I know anyone.

Sadly, our standards for being part of a church remain at the same level as our connection to fellow fliers. Worship services bring people together in the same space to worship as a glorious anticipation of heaven, but they don't allow us to know or be known. That's why I believe small groups and Bible study classes create siblings. Still, even in smaller settings, connections with believers aren't automatic. When it comes to relationships, you reap what you sow. If you keep your guard up, gathering will become another religious chore. But when you open up your life, others are more likely to open theirs.

Pastors and staff members can make opportunities for you to connect, but you must do the hard work of investing in relationships. Doing so will require you to put away self-centered, individualistic tendencies. If a thousand people enter an auditorium on a Sunday morning pursuing their own preferences, the church will decay quickly. But imagine twenty gathered people who "submit to one another out of reverence for Christ" (Eph 5:21 NIV). Imagine the teaching and ministry that could take place. Imagine a group of servants who spur one another on. Who, together, carve away buried sinful tendencies lodged deep within the flesh. Who worship from the heart without the need to impress each other. Imagine a church family.

Along the way, I tried to avoid excessive idealism. Relationships take work, and even the closest families face conflict. If we're going to fight, though, our priority should be to fight like siblings, not enemies. Christian siblings acknowledge daily that they battle sin, not flesh and blood. Like Paul in the book of Romans, I sometimes like to personify sin to make the point.[5] "We refuse to let Mr. Sin divide us!" Mr. Sin will coax us to battle with weapons that produce the most collateral damage—harming relationships, families, and hearts along with the intended enemy. He wants believers to condemn one another in the court of public opinion so that trust is lost. Mr. Sin intends to muddy the gospel by pitting Christians against one another on social media or publicizing church splits. Paul's words are as relevant as ever. He warns in Romans 6:12–13 (CSB), "Therefore do not let sin reign in your mortal body, so that you obey its desires. And do not offer any parts of it to sin as weapons for unrighteousness. But as those who are alive from the dead, offer yourselves to God, and all the parts of yourselves to God as weapons for righteousness." For whose team will we fight when conflict arises?

Inevitably, conflict causes some to fly and others to fight. For the fliers, I beg you to put all of your energy into working out the conflict before you consider leaving your church family. Local church families are like a good steak. Steak requires a combination of simple ingredients and simple cooking. Salt, pepper, and a low-temperature grill can do wonders. But overdo any of these elements, and you'll ruin dinner. Because I am a terrible cook, I have burned and oversalted more T-bones than I would like to admit. The same mistakes can ruin church life. Churches taste great with a healthy balance of vocal leaders and joyful servants, extroverts and introverts, the bold and the cautious, and so on. Overseason with any of these ingredients, and a local church might offend the palate. Some congregations even become toxic. At that point, flying might be the only option.

If you must leave, don't shop for your next church (leaving the steak analogy behind). Date a local church or a few, if necessary. Search for a family that will not only serve your needs but that also needs your God-given gifts. Find a family to join, not a place to attend. The church dating process will require more time than shopping. After all, it took my wife much longer to decide to marry me than it takes her to choose the right avocado. Invest in a local church for a season, serving and participating in church life as

5. See Rom 6:14, where Paul presents sin as a slave master.

much as possible. Only then will you begin to think of them as people—as siblings—rather than as your own spiritual service representatives. Yes, it might be awkward to break it off after six months, but at least you can know before saying "I do."

A final word for church members: treat pastors with respect, grace, and generosity. Not idolatry. Keep God on the throne. Only he is holy and faithful.

For the Shepherds

The ministry calling presents more complex challenges than the average church member will ever recognize. For many pastors, work becomes an all-day, everyday grind. Needy people don't keep banker's hours. Ministry leaders face budget constraints, staff conflicts, the endless barrage of well-meaning opinions, and a personal sense of hypocrisy when their own spiritual walks aren't up to snuff. Then there's the ministry roller coaster. One minute you're congratulating the parents of a beautiful newborn baby. The next minute, you visit the family who just placed their loved one on hospice. You head back to the office to sculpt a Spirit-led sermon only to receive a phone call from a long-time member offended by his small group leader's political stances. Finally, you head home to a family who wants to enjoy your presence while you fight to keep your head and heart in the room. The ups and downs of the average day can be dizzying.

I offer no solution to the ministry roller coaster, but I believe that implementing the family model can relieve some of the pressure of ministry. For one, family-oriented pastors value relationships over tasks. I don't mean they avoid tasks, letting the church building crumble and worship services descend into chaos. But their tasks are always a means to a relational end. Let's assess for a minute. Do you hide in your office with an Excel sheet on the screen because you prefer to avoid your church family? Or do you meticulously comb through a budget because you want to save every possible dollar for ministry—for discipling the family and reaching the lost with the gospel? Do you spend twenty hours each week studying for a sermon because you want to be alone? Or do you study hard because your brothers and sisters are starving for truth? The reason behind a task matters. That's why Paul demanded that the Corinthians give cheerfully (2 Cor 9:7). The begrudging giver does the same task, but his effort doesn't translate into worship. The cheerful giver meets the needs of the Christian family in a manner that glorifies the Father. Likewise, the minister who works tirelessly for the edification of his siblings, valuing them more than the task, exalts the Father.

Another way to reduce ministry pressure is to find a family within the family. One question should reveal whether you need to make some changes. Does anybody in your congregation know the real you? Consider whether you regularly share your internal struggles and victories with any church member outside of your spouse. For some, opening up comes naturally. Their life is an open book that anyone can read. Others, myself included, prefer to keep that book shut tight and hidden under the couch. Transparency requires trust, a fleeting commodity for many of us in ministry. But we'll never become a family without trust. So find a group of people to open up to, to trust with the imperfection that is your life. Be wise but not closed.

A third ministry stressor is church lust. We ogle the church across the street that seems to have it all, knowing that we would feel unbridled joy if we served a congregation like that. Usually, our lustful eyes zero in on budgets, attendance numbers, facilities, or staff sizes. But some simply want a congregation that isn't fighting for power but is relatively healthy. Or maybe someone else's worship team is better. Whatever the case, church lust leads to dissatisfaction, and dissatisfaction to selfish leadership, and selfish leadership to a critical spirit, and a critical spirit to joyless slavery to a paycheck. I truly believe that church lust is rampant among pastors and is a leading cause of ministry ineffectiveness and eventual burnout. So, once again, if the church is a family, I beg you to love the one you're with.

For Everyone

This book has offered no silver bullet. We began by admitting that our thinking determines our doing, even in church life. Along the way, we saw the biblical roots of the familial metaphor and compared it to the corporate-church model that has invaded American churches in recent decades. The close of each chapter has provided practical ideas for changing our thinking patterns to match the biblical model of the church family. Yet, every church is different. What works in one church family might fail in another. That's why God has put you in your local church. He wants you to evaluate every aspect of church life with the biblical vision of the family of God as your guide. So, let me offer a few additional questions to get you started.

Does your worship music use sibling language or even address the church as a whole, or is each song focused only on the individual? Do sermons and lessons ever emphasize the doctrine of familification—that the gospel creates a family? What do your membership processes reveal about what it means to be part of a church? Do membership expectations look more like an employee performance checklist or like the unspoken values of a committed family? Have you ever defined what success looks like for your church? If so, does your articulation of success look more like that of a credit card company or like the desires of parents for their newborn? Do you merely copy the practices of a seemingly more successful local church family? Or does the Spirit have the authority to lead your church in a way that meets the unique needs of your brothers and sisters?

I have hope for the future. I hope de-churched people will love the church again, longing for the commitment and affection they witness between believers. I hope church life will become a bridge to the gospel, not a wall. No more "I like Jesus but hate churches" but, instead, "Look at how they love one another!" I hope pastors will love the ministry because of the siblings they serve. I hope ministry leaders will find joy in the spiritual growth of others whether numbers increase or not. I hope members will think first about how to serve their brothers and sisters. I hope musicians will write songs about the family of God, and authors will pen blogs and books. Mostly, I hope the Father will be exalted as he watches his children love one another.

"Let brotherly love continue" (Heb 13:1 CSB).

Bibliography

Aasgaard, Reidar. *"My Beloved Brothers and Sisters!": Christian Siblingship in Paul.* JSNTSS 265. New York: T&T Clark, 2004.

Associated Press. "Burger King Ditches 'Have It Your Way' Slogan." *Fox News*, May 20, 2014; last revised Nov. 22, 2016. https://www.foxnews.com/food-drink/burger-king-ditches-have-it-your-way-slogan.

Bartchy, S. Scott. "Undermining Ancient Patriarchy: The Apostle Paul's Vision of a Society of Siblings." *Biblical Theology Journal* 29, no. 2 (1999) 68–78.

Behesti, Naz. "The Detrimental Effect of Loneliness on Your Health and What You Can Do about It." *Forbes*, May 31, 2019. https://www.forbes.com/sites/nazbeheshti/2019/05/31/the-detrimental-effect-of-loneliness-on-your-health-and-what-you-can-do-about-it/#65810573d1ae.

Botelho, Elena Lytkina, et al. "What Sets Successful CEOs Apart." *Harvard Business Review* (May/June 2017) 70–77.

Burke, Trevor J. *Adopted into God's Family: Exploring a Pauline Metaphor.* NSBT 22. Downers Grove, IL: IVP, 2006.

———. *Family Matters: A Socio-Historical Study of Kinship Metaphors in First Thessalonians.* JSNTSS 247. New York: T&T Clark, 2003.

Cheung, Alex T. *Idol Food in Corinth: Jewish Background and Pauline Legacy.* JSNTSS 176. Sheffield, UK: Sheffield Academic, 1999.

Cohen, Stacey. "Appliances Really Don't Last As Long As They Used To." Consumer Affairs, Feb. 17, 2015. https://www.consumeraffairs.com/news/appliances-really-dont-last-as-long-as-they-used-to-021715.html.

Darr, Katheryn Pfisterer. *Isaiah's Vision and the Family of God.* Louisville: Westminster John Knox, 1994.

Davenport, David, and Gordon Lloyd. *Rugged Individualism: Dead or Alive?* Stanford, CA: Hoover Institution Press, 2016.

deSilva, David A. "Third and Fourth Maccabees." In *Dictionary of New Testament Background*, edited by Craig A. Evans and Stanley Porter, 661–66. Downers Grove, IL: IVP, 2000.

Dodd, Patton. "Low-Income Communities Are Struggling to Support Churches." *Atlantic*, Jan. 7, 2018. https://www.theatlantic.com/politics/archive/2018/01/low-income-communities-churches/549677/.

Food and Drug Administration. "Food Defect Levels Handbook." Last updated Sept. 7, 2018. https://www.fda.gov/food/ingredients-additives-gras-packaging-guidance-documents-regulatory-information/food-defect-levels-handbook.

"The Four P's of Church Marketing." No to the Quo, Mar. 14, 2011. https://www.notothequo.com/the-4ps-of-church-marketing/.

Garland, David E. "The Dispute over Food Sacrificed to Idols (1 Cor 8:1–11:1)." *Perspectives in Religious Studies* 30, no. 2 (Summer 2003) 173–97.

Gaventa, Beverly Roberts. *Our Mother Saint Paul.* Louisville: Westminster John Knox, 2007.

Gorodnichenko, Yuriy, and Gerard Roland. "Understanding the Individualism-Collectivism Cleavage and Its Effects: Lessons from Cultural Psychology." In *Institutions and Comparative Economic Development,* edited by Masahiko Aoki et al., 213–36. International Economic Association. London: Palgrave Macmillan, 2012.

Gray, Patrick. "Brotherly Love and High Priestly Christology." *Journal of Biblical Literature* 122, no. 2 (2003) 335–51.

Hanbury, Mary. "Meet the Waltons: How America's Wealthiest Family Spends its Walmart Fortune." *Business Insider,* Aug. 16, 2018. https://www.businessinsider.com/how-the-waltons-spend-their-fortune-2017-7.

Hellerman, Joseph H. *The Ancient Church as Family.* Minneapolis: Fortress, 2001.

————. *When the Church Was a Family: Recapturing Jesus' Vision for Authentic Christian Community.* Nashville: B&H, 2009.

Hess, Richard S., and M. Daniel Carroll R, eds. *Family in the Bible: Exploring Customs, Culture, and Context.* Grand Rapids: Baker, 2003.

Hilgemann, Brandon. "The Best Leadership Books for Pastors." Sept. 11, 2013. https://www.propreacher.com/best-leadership-books-for-pastors/.

Hylen, Susan E. "Metaphor Matters: Violence and Ethics in Revelation." *Catholic Biblical Quarterly* 73 (2011) 777–96.

Infograpics in Leaders and Pastors. "The Ups and Downs of Ministry." Barna, Aug. 7, 2018. https://www.barna.com/research/ups-downs-ministry/?utm_source=Barna+Update+List&utm_campaign=fe4baf7a74-EMAIL_CAMPAIGN_2017_12_28_COPY_01&utm_medium=email&utm_term=0_8560a0e52e-fe4baf7a74-180576733&mc_cid=fe4baf7a74&mc_eid=8170d57853.

Jarvie, Jenny. "Averting an Ultraconservative Takeover, Southern Baptists Elect a New Leader." *LA Times,* June 15, 2021. https://www.latimes.com/world-nation/story/2021-06-15/southern-baptist-convention-nashville.

Jeffers, James S. *The Greco-Roman World of the New Testament Era: Exploring the Background of Early Christianity.* Downers Grove, IL: IVP, 1999.

Jethani, Skye, *Immeasurable: Reflections on the Soul of Ministry in the Age of Church, Inc.* Chicago: Moody, 2017.

Jones, Jeffrey M. "U.S. Church Membership Down Sharply in Past Two Decades." *Gallup,* Apr. 18, 2019. https://news.gallup.com/poll/248837/church-membership-down-sharply-past-two-decades.aspx?g_source=link_WWWV9&g_medium=SEARCH&g_campaign=item_&g_content=U.S.%2520Church%2520Membership%2520Down%2520Sharply%2520in%2520Past%2520Two%2520Decades.

Kaiser, Walter C. *Preaching and Teaching from the Old Testament: A Guide for the Church.* Grand Rapids: Baker, 2003.

Lakoff, George, and Mark Johnson. *Metaphors We Live By.* Chicago: University of Chicago Press, 1980.

Lavietes, Stuart. "Rev. Robert Schuller, Eighty-Eight, Dies; Built an Empire Preaching Self-Belief." *NY Times,* Apr. 2, 2015. https://www.nytimes.com/2015/04/03/us/rev-robert-h-schuller-hour-of-power-evangelist-dies-at-88.html.

"Loneliness Research." Campaign to End Loneliness. https://www.campaigntoendlone liness.org/loneliness-research/.

Luther, Martin. "Lord, Keep Us Steadfast In Thy Word." https://hymnary.org/text/lord_ keep_us_steadfast_in_your_word.

———. "A Mighty Fortress." https://hymnary.org/text/a_mighty_fortress_is_our_god_a _bulwark.

Malina, Bruce. *Christian Origins and Cultural Anthropology.* Atlanta: John Knox, 1986.

McGavran, Donald A. *Understanding Church Growth.* 3rd ed. Grand Rapids: Eerdmans, 1990.

McIntosh Gary L., ed. *Evaluating the Church Growth Movement: Five Views.* Grand Rapids: Zondervan, 2004.

McKnight, Scot. *Galatians.* NIVAC 9. Grand Rapids: Zondervan, 1995.

———. "Willow Creek, What's a Pastor?" *Jesus Creed* (blog), Sept. 16, 2019. https:// www.patheos.com/blogs/jesuscreed/2019/09/16/willow-creek-whats-a-pastor/.

McNeel, Jennifer Houston. *Paul as Infant and Nursing Mother: Metaphor, Rhetoric, and Identity in 1 Thessalonians 2:5–8.* SBL Early Christianity and Its Literature 12. Atlanta: SBL, 2014.

Minnicks, Margaret. "Largest Churches in America and How They Grew So Quickly." Owlcation, Feb. 8, 2019. https://owlcation.com/humanities/The-Largest-Churches-in-America-and-How-They-Got-That-Way.

Moo, Douglas J. *Galatians.* BECNT. Grand Rapids: Baker, 2013.

Moxnes, Halvor, ed. *Constructing Early Christian Families: Family as Social Reality and Metaphor.* London: Routledge, 1997.

Murphy, Simon. "I Was a Successful Church Planter and It Almost Ruined Me (Part 2)." Redeemer City to City, June 21, 2018. https://medium.com/redeemer-city-to-city/i-was-a-successful-church-planter-and-it-almost-ruined-me-part-2-cd3fcec31ab0.

Peeler, Amy B. *You Are My Son: The Family of God in the Epistle to the Hebrews.* LNTS. London: T&T Clark, 2015.

Peppard, Michael. "Brother Against Brother: *Controversiae* about Inheritance Disputes and 1 Corinthians 6:1–11." *Journal of Biblical Literature* 133, no. 1 (2014) 179–92.

Persaud, Michael. "Creating a Clear Church Marketing Strategy." Church Brand Guide, Jan. 23, 2019. https://churchbrandguide.com/creating-a-clear-church-marketing-strategy/.

Rainer, Thom. *The Book of Church Growth: History, Theology, and Principles.* Nashville: Broadman, 1993.

Resnick, Brian. "Loneliness Actually Hurts." Vox, Jan. 30, 2017. https://www.vox.com/ science-and-health/2017/1/30/14219498/loneliness-hurts.

Richards, E. Randolph, and Brandon J. O'Brien. *Misreading Scripture with Western Eyes: Removing Cultural Blinders to Better Understand the Bible.* Downers Grove: IVP, 2012.

Roach, David. "Platt's McLean Bible Church Hit with Attempted Takeover, Lawsuit from Opposition." *Christianity Today,* July 22, 2021. https://www.christianitytoday.com/ news/2021/july/david-platt-mclean-bible-church-elder-race-politics-critics.html.

Sandnes, Karl Olav. *A New Family: Conversion and Ecclesiology in the Early Church, with Cross-Cultural Comparisons.* Studies in the Intercultural History of Christianity 91. New York: Peter Lang, 1994.

Schreiner, Thomas R. *First Corinthians: An Introduction and Commentary*. TNTC 7. Downers Grove, IL: IVP, 2018.

Schuller, Robert A. *When You Are Down to Nothing, God Is Up to Something: Discovering Divine Purpose and Provision When Life Hurts*. New York: FaithWords, 2011.

Schuller, Robert H. *Your Church Has Real Possibilities*. Glendale, CA: Gospel Light, 1974.

Segler, Franklin M., and Randall Bradley. *Christian Worship: Its Theology and Practice*. 3rd ed. Nashville: B&H, 2006.

Sexton, Jason S. "Introduction: Recalibrating the Church's Mission." In *Four Views on the Church's Mission*, edited by Jason S. Sexton, 7–16. Grand Rapids: Zondervan, 2017.

Soper, Taylor. "Amazon Now Employs Nearly 1.3 Million People Worldwide after Adding 500,000 Workers in 2020." Geekwire, Feb. 2, 2021. https://www.geekwire.com/2021/amazon-now-employs-nearly-1-3-million-people-worldwide-adding-500000-workers-2020/.

Stanley, Andy. *Deep and Wide: Creating Churches Unchurched People Love to Attend*. Grand Rapids: Zondervan, 2012.

Stetzer, Ed. "How Protestant Pastors Spend Their Time." *Christianity Today*, Dec. 2009. https://www.christianitytoday.com/edstetzer/2009/december/how-protestant-pastors-spend-their-time.html. Site discontinued.

Susek, Ron. *Firestorm: Preventing and Overcoming Church Conflicts*. Grand Rapids: Baker, 1999.

Tomlinson, F. Alan. "The Purpose and Stewardship Theme within the Pastoral Epistles." In *Entrusted with the Gospel: Paul's Theology in the Pastoral Epistles*, edited by Andreas J. Köstenberger and Terry L. Wilder, 52–83. Nashville: B&H, 2010.

Tverberg, Lois. *Walking in the Dust of Rabbi Jesus: How the Jewish Words of Jesus Can Change Your Life*. Grand Rapids: Zondervan, 2012.

Vanderbloemen. "Willow Creek Community Church Senior Pastor." Accessed Sept. 16, 2019. https://www.vanderbloemen.com/job/willow-creek-community-church-senior-pastor. Site discontinued.

Van Yperen, Jim. *Making Peace: A Guide to Overcoming Church Conflict*. Chicago: Moody, 2008.

de Villiers, Pieter G. R. "Safe in the Family of God: Soteriological Perspectives in 1 Thessalonians." In *Salvation in the New Testament: Perspectives on Soteriology*, edited by Jan G. van der Watt, 305–30. Novum Testamentum Supplements 121. Boston: Brill, 2005.

Wagner, C. Peter. *Leading Your Church to Growth: The Secret of Pastor/People Partnership in Dynamic Church Growth*. Venture, CA: Regal, 1982.

———. *Strategies for Church Growth: Tools for Effective Mission and Evangelism*. Venture, CA: Regal, 1989.

"Where Does Chocolate Come From?" National Confectioners Association. https://www.candyusa.com/story-of-chocolate/where-does-chocolate-come-from/.

Wilson, Jared C. *The Prodigal Church: A Gentle Manifesto against the Status Quo*. Wheaton, IL: Crossway, 2015.

Winter, B. W. "Civil Litigation in Secular Corinth and the Church: The Forensic Background to 1 Corinthians 6:1–8." *New Testament Studies* 37 (1991) 559–72.

Zamora, Stephenie. "How to Handle Life When Everyone Has an Opinion about What You're Doing." *Huffington Post*, Mar. 7, 2014; updated Dec. 6, 2017. https://www.huffpost.com/entry/how-to-handle-life-when-e_n_4920116.

CPSIA information can be obtained
at www.ICGtesting.com
Printed in the USA
JSHW020756090222
22666JS00004B/10